C-3605   CAREER EXAMINATION SERIES

This is your
PASSBOOK for...

Customer Service/ Information Representative

Test Preparation Study Guide
Questions & Answers

COPYRIGHT NOTICE

This book is SOLELY intended for, is sold ONLY to, and its use is RESTRICTED to individual, bona fide applicants or candidates who qualify by virtue of having seriously filed applications for appropriate license, certificate, professional and/or promotional advancement, higher school matriculation, scholarship, or other legitimate requirements of education and/or governmental authorities.

This book is NOT intended for use, class instruction, tutoring, training, duplication, copying, reprinting, excerption, or adaptation, etc., by:

1) Other publishers
2) Proprietors and/or Instructors of "Coaching" and/or Preparatory Courses
3) Personnel and/or Training Divisions of commercial, industrial, and governmental organizations
4) Schools, colleges, or universities and/or their departments and staffs, including teachers and other personnel
5) Testing Agencies or Bureaus
6) Study groups which seek by the purchase of a single volume to copy and/or duplicate and/or adapt this material for use by the group as a whole without having purchased individual volumes for each of the members of the group
7) Et al.

Such persons would be in violation of appropriate Federal and State statutes.

PROVISION OF LICENSING AGREEMENTS – Recognized educational, commercial, industrial, and governmental institutions and organizations, and others legitimately engaged in educational pursuits, including training, testing, and measurement activities, may address request for a licensing agreement to the copyright owners, who will determine whether, and under what conditions, including fees and charges, the materials in this book may be used them. In other words, a licensing facility exists for the legitimate use of the material in this book on other than an individual basis. However, it is asseverated and affirmed here that the material in this book CANNOT be used without the receipt of the express permission of such a licensing agreement from the Publishers. Inquiries re licensing should be addressed to the company, attention rights and permissions department.

All rights reserved, including the right of reproduction in whole or in part, in any form or by any means, electronic or mechanical, including photocopying, recording, or by any information storage and retrieval system, without permission in writing from the Publisher.

Copyright © 2024 by
National Learning Corporation

212 Michael Drive, Syosset, NY 11791
(516) 921-8888 • www.passbooks.com
E-mail: info@passbooks.com

PUBLISHED IN THE UNITED STATES OF AMERICA

PASSBOOK® SERIES

THE *PASSBOOK® SERIES* has been created to prepare applicants and candidates for the ultimate academic battlefield – the examination room.

At some time in our lives, each and every one of us may be required to take an examination – for validation, matriculation, admission, qualification, registration, certification, or licensure.

Based on the assumption that every applicant or candidate has met the basic formal educational standards, has taken the required number of courses, and read the necessary texts, the *PASSBOOK® SERIES* furnishes the one special preparation which may assure passing with confidence, instead of failing with insecurity. Examination questions – together with answers – are furnished as the basic vehicle for study so that the mysteries of the examination and its compounding difficulties may be eliminated or diminished by a sure method.

This book is meant to help you pass your examination provided that you qualify and are serious in your objective.

The entire field is reviewed through the huge store of content information which is succinctly presented through a provocative and challenging approach – the question-and-answer method.

A climate of success is established by furnishing the correct answers at the end of each test.

You soon learn to recognize types of questions, forms of questions, and patterns of questioning. You may even begin to anticipate expected outcomes.

You perceive that many questions are repeated or adapted so that you can gain acute insights, which may enable you to score many sure points.

You learn how to confront new questions, or types of questions, and to attack them confidently and work out the correct answers.

You note objectives and emphases, and recognize pitfalls and dangers, so that you may make positive educational adjustments.

Moreover, you are kept fully informed in relation to new concepts, methods, practices, and directions in the field.

You discover that you are actually taking the examination all the time: you are preparing for the examination by "taking" an examination, not by reading extraneous and/or supererogatory textbooks.

In short, this PASSBOOK®, used directedly, should be an important factor in helping you to pass your test.

CUSTOMER SERVICE/INFORMATION REPRESENTATIVE

DUTIES:
   Customer Service/Information Representatives provide customer service utilizing computer databases and information technology to access information required for responses and overseeing customer service work; record, track, respond to, and resolve telephone, email and/or walk-in inquiries in an agency customer service center, agency help desk, or other agency customer service unit; provide information, record complaints and requests, and conduct research to resolve problems; forward unresolved matters to appropriate staff and offices for further action; enter customer information and inquiries into a computer tracking system; perform related clerical administrative tasks and computer support work. All Customer Information Representatives perform related work.

TYPICAL WORK ACTIVITIES:
   Answers telephone, mail, email and in-person inquiries and determines service required; requests customer information needed to respond to inquires; records customer information, inquiries, and resolutions in tracking systems; receives payments and fees, processes and generates payments and adjusts records accordingly; refers complex requests for reply; keeps customers apprised of status and progress on unresolved service requests; answers routine, frequently asked and scripted questions, and provides information about services; prepares written replies using forms and form letters; updates inquiry tracking system to reflect actions taken, responses given and inquiries forwarded for further research and response; updates reference and source data and tables in agency Information Technology systems; uses computer databases and information technology systems to research information needed to respond to and track the progress of responses to telephone, mail, email, and in-person inquiries; enters customer information into databases to update personal records and accounts; aids less experienced Customer Information Representatives in mastering procedures and systems.

SCOPE OF THE EXAMINATION:
   The multiple-choice test is designed to assess the extent to which candidates have certain abilities determined to important to the performance of the tasks of a Customer Service/Information Representative. The test may include questions on understanding and interpreting written information; customer service situations, principles and practices including telling when something is wrong or likely to go wrong, and identifying the whole problem as well as the elements of the problem; combining separate pieces of information to form a general conclusion; applying general rules to a specific situation. The test may include questions requiring the use of any of the following abilities:
Inductive Reasoning - The ability to combine separate pieces of information or specific answers to problems to form general rules or conclusions; to think of possible reasons for why things go together. Example: A Customer Service/Information Representative may use this ability when utilizing databases and information technology to access information when responding to complaints and requests.
Written Comprehension - The ability to understand written sentences and paragraphs. Example: A Customer Service/Information Representative may use this ability when conducting research to resolve customer problems.
Written Expression - The ability to use English words or sentences in writing so that others will understand. Example: A Customer Service/Information Representative may use this ability to enter customer information and inquiries into computer tracking systems, or perform related clerical administrative tasks.

HOW TO TAKE A TEST

I. YOU MUST PASS AN EXAMINATION

A. *WHAT EVERY CANDIDATE SHOULD KNOW*

Examination applicants often ask us for help in preparing for the written test. What can I study in advance? What kinds of questions will be asked? How will the test be given? How will the papers be graded?

As an applicant for a civil service examination, you may be wondering about some of these things. Our purpose here is to suggest effective methods of advance study and to describe civil service examinations.

Your chances for success on this examination can be increased if you know how to prepare. Those "pre-examination jitters" can be reduced if you know what to expect. You can even experience an adventure in good citizenship if you know why civil service exams are given.

B. *WHY ARE CIVIL SERVICE EXAMINATIONS GIVEN?*

Civil service examinations are important to you in two ways. As a citizen, you want public jobs filled by employees who know how to do their work. As a job seeker, you want a fair chance to compete for that job on an equal footing with other candidates. The best-known means of accomplishing this two-fold goal is the competitive examination.

Exams are widely publicized throughout the nation. They may be administered for jobs in federal, state, city, municipal, town or village governments or agencies.

Any citizen may apply, with some limitations, such as the age or residence of applicants. Your experience and education may be reviewed to see whether you meet the requirements for the particular examination. When these requirements exist, they are reasonable and applied consistently to all applicants. Thus, a competitive examination may cause you some uneasiness now, but it is your privilege and safeguard.

C. *HOW ARE CIVIL SERVICE EXAMS DEVELOPED?*

Examinations are carefully written by trained technicians who are specialists in the field known as "psychological measurement," in consultation with recognized authorities in the field of work that the test will cover. These experts recommend the subject matter areas or skills to be tested; only those knowledges or skills important to your success on the job are included. The most reliable books and source materials available are used as references. Together, the experts and technicians judge the difficulty level of the questions.

Test technicians know how to phrase questions so that the problem is clearly stated. Their ethics do not permit "trick" or "catch" questions. Questions may have been tried out on sample groups, or subjected to statistical analysis, to determine their usefulness.

Written tests are often used in combination with performance tests, ratings of training and experience, and oral interviews. All of these measures combine to form the best-known means of finding the right person for the right job.

II. HOW TO PASS THE WRITTEN TEST

A. NATURE OF THE EXAMINATION

To prepare intelligently for civil service examinations, you should know how they differ from school examinations you have taken. In school you were assigned certain definite pages to read or subjects to cover. The examination questions were quite detailed and usually emphasized memory. Civil service exams, on the other hand, try to discover your present ability to perform the duties of a position, plus your potentiality to learn these duties. In other words, a civil service exam attempts to predict how successful you will be. Questions cover such a broad area that they cannot be as minute and detailed as school exam questions.

In the public service similar kinds of work, or positions, are grouped together in one "class." This process is known as *position-classification*. All the positions in a class are paid according to the salary range for that class. One class title covers all of these positions, and they are all tested by the same examination.

B. FOUR BASIC STEPS

1) Study the announcement

How, then, can you know what subjects to study? Our best answer is: "Learn as much as possible about the class of positions for which you've applied." The exam will test the knowledge, skills and abilities needed to do the work.

Your most valuable source of information about the position you want is the official exam announcement. This announcement lists the training and experience qualifications. Check these standards and apply only if you come reasonably close to meeting them.

The brief description of the position in the examination announcement offers some clues to the subjects which will be tested. Think about the job itself. Review the duties in your mind. Can you perform them, or are there some in which you are rusty? Fill in the blank spots in your preparation.

Many jurisdictions preview the written test in the exam announcement by including a section called "Knowledge and Abilities Required," "Scope of the Examination," or some similar heading. Here you will find out specifically what fields will be tested.

2) Review your own background

Once you learn in general what the position is all about, and what you need to know to do the work, ask yourself which subjects you already know fairly well and which need improvement. You may wonder whether to concentrate on improving your strong areas or on building some background in your fields of weakness. When the announcement has specified "some knowledge" or "considerable knowledge," or has used adjectives like "beginning principles of..." or "advanced ... methods," you can get a clue as to the number and difficulty of questions to be asked in any given field. More questions, and hence broader coverage, would be included for those subjects which are more important in the work. Now weigh your strengths and weaknesses against the job requirements and prepare accordingly.

3) Determine the level of the position

Another way to tell how intensively you should prepare is to understand the level of the job for which you are applying. Is it the entering level? In other words, is this the position in which beginners in a field of work are hired? Or is it an intermediate or advanced level? Sometimes this is indicated by such words as "Junior" or "Senior" in the class title. Other jurisdictions use Roman numerals to designate the level – Clerk I, Clerk II, for example. The word "Supervisor" sometimes appears in the title. If the level is not indicated by the title, check the description of duties. Will you be working under very close supervision, or will you have responsibility for independent decisions in this work?

4) Choose appropriate study materials

Now that you know the subjects to be examined and the relative amount of each subject to be covered, you can choose suitable study materials. For beginning level jobs, or even advanced ones, if you have a pronounced weakness in some aspect of your training, read a modern, standard textbook in that field. Be sure it is up to date and has general coverage. Such books are normally available at your library, and the librarian will be glad to help you locate one. For entry-level positions, questions of appropriate difficulty are chosen – neither highly advanced questions, nor those too simple. Such questions require careful thought but not advanced training.

If the position for which you are applying is technical or advanced, you will read more advanced, specialized material. If you are already familiar with the basic principles of your field, elementary textbooks would waste your time. Concentrate on advanced textbooks and technical periodicals. Think through the concepts and review difficult problems in your field.

These are all general sources. You can get more ideas on your own initiative, following these leads. For example, training manuals and publications of the government agency which employs workers in your field can be useful, particularly for technical and professional positions. A letter or visit to the government department involved may result in more specific study suggestions, and certainly will provide you with a more definite idea of the exact nature of the position you are seeking.

III. KINDS OF TESTS

Tests are used for purposes other than measuring knowledge and ability to perform specified duties. For some positions, it is equally important to test ability to make adjustments to new situations or to profit from training. In others, basic mental abilities not dependent on information are essential. Questions which test these things may not appear as pertinent to the duties of the position as those which test for knowledge and information. Yet they are often highly important parts of a fair examination. For very general questions, it is almost impossible to help you direct your study efforts. What we can do is to point out some of the more common of these general abilities needed in public service positions and describe some typical questions.

1) General information

Broad, general information has been found useful for predicting job success in some kinds of work. This is tested in a variety of ways, from vocabulary lists to questions about current events. Basic background in some field of work, such as sociology or economics, may be sampled in a group of questions. Often these are principles which have become familiar to most persons through exposure rather than through formal training. It is difficult to advise you how to study for these questions; being alert to the world around you is our best suggestion.

2) Verbal ability

An example of an ability needed in many positions is verbal or language ability. Verbal ability is, in brief, the ability to use and understand words. Vocabulary and grammar tests are typical measures of this ability. Reading comprehension or paragraph interpretation questions are common in many kinds of civil service tests. You are given a paragraph of written material and asked to find its central meaning.

3) Numerical ability

Number skills can be tested by the familiar arithmetic problem, by checking paired lists of numbers to see which are alike and which are different, or by interpreting charts and graphs. In the latter test, a graph may be printed in the test booklet which you are asked to use as the basis for answering questions.

4) Observation

A popular test for law-enforcement positions is the observation test. A picture is shown to you for several minutes, then taken away. Questions about the picture test your ability to observe both details and larger elements.

5) Following directions

In many positions in the public service, the employee must be able to carry out written instructions dependably and accurately. You may be given a chart with several columns, each column listing a variety of information. The questions require you to carry out directions involving the information given in the chart.

6) Skills and aptitudes

Performance tests effectively measure some manual skills and aptitudes. When the skill is one in which you are trained, such as typing or shorthand, you can practice. These tests are often very much like those given in business school or high school courses. For many of the other skills and aptitudes, however, no short-time preparation can be made. Skills and abilities natural to you or that you have developed throughout your lifetime are being tested.

Many of the general questions just described provide all the data needed to answer the questions and ask you to use your reasoning ability to find the answers. Your best preparation for these tests, as well as for tests of facts and ideas, is to be at your physical and mental best. You, no doubt, have your own methods of getting into an exam-taking mood and keeping "in shape." The next section lists some ideas on this subject.

IV. KINDS OF QUESTIONS

Only rarely is the "essay" question, which you answer in narrative form, used in civil service tests. Civil service tests are usually of the short-answer type. Full instructions for answering these questions will be given to you at the examination. But in case this is your first experience with short-answer questions and separate answer sheets, here is what you need to know:

1) **Multiple-choice Questions**

Most popular of the short-answer questions is the "multiple choice" or "best answer" question. It can be used, for example, to test for factual knowledge, ability to solve problems or judgment in meeting situations found at work.

A multiple-choice question is normally one of three types—
- It can begin with an incomplete statement followed by several possible endings. You are to find the one ending which *best* completes the statement, although some of the others may not be entirely wrong.
- It can also be a complete statement in the form of a question which is answered by choosing one of the statements listed.

- It can be in the form of a problem – again you select the best answer.

Here is an example of a multiple-choice question with a discussion which should give you some clues as to the method for choosing the right answer:

When an employee has a complaint about his assignment, the action which will *best* help him overcome his difficulty is to
- A. discuss his difficulty with his coworkers
- B. take the problem to the head of the organization
- C. take the problem to the person who gave him the assignment
- D. say nothing to anyone about his complaint

In answering this question, you should study each of the choices to find which is best. Consider choice "A" – Certainly an employee may discuss his complaint with fellow employees, but no change or improvement can result, and the complaint remains unresolved. Choice "B" is a poor choice since the head of the organization probably does not know what assignment you have been given, and taking your problem to him is known as "going over the head" of the supervisor. The supervisor, or person who made the assignment, is the person who can clarify it or correct any injustice. Choice "C" is, therefore, correct. To say nothing, as in choice "D," is unwise. Supervisors have and interest in knowing the problems employees are facing, and the employee is seeking a solution to his problem.

2) True/False Questions

The "true/false" or "right/wrong" form of question is sometimes used. Here a complete statement is given. Your job is to decide whether the statement is right or wrong.

SAMPLE: A roaming cell-phone call to a nearby city costs less than a non-roaming call to a distant city.

This statement is wrong, or false, since roaming calls are more expensive.

This is not a complete list of all possible question forms, although most of the others are variations of these common types. You will always get complete directions for answering questions. Be sure you understand *how* to mark your answers – ask questions until you do.

V. RECORDING YOUR ANSWERS

Computer terminals are used more and more today for many different kinds of exams.
For an examination with very few applicants, you may be told to record your answers in the test booklet itself. Separate answer sheets are much more common. If this separate answer sheet is to be scored by machine – and this is often the case – it is highly important that you mark your answers correctly in order to get credit.
An electronic scoring machine is often used in civil service offices because of the speed with which papers can be scored. Machine-scored answer sheets must be marked with a pencil, which will be given to you. This pencil has a high graphite content which responds to the electronic scoring machine. As a matter of fact, stray dots may register as answers, so do not let your pencil rest on the answer sheet while you are pondering the correct answer. Also, if your pencil lead breaks or is otherwise defective, ask for another.

Since the answer sheet will be dropped in a slot in the scoring machine, be careful not to bend the corners or get the paper crumpled.

The answer sheet normally has five vertical columns of numbers, with 30 numbers to a column. These numbers correspond to the question numbers in your test booklet. After each number, going across the page are four or five pairs of dotted lines. These short dotted lines have small letters or numbers above them. The first two pairs may also have a "T" or "F" above the letters. This indicates that the first two pairs only are to be used if the questions are of the true-false type. If the questions are multiple choice, disregard the "T" and "F" and pay attention only to the small letters or numbers.

Answer your questions in the manner of the sample that follows:

32. The largest city in the United States is
    A. Washington, D.C.
    B. New York City
    C. Chicago
    D. Detroit
    E. San Francisco

1) Choose the answer you think is best. (New York City is the largest, so "B" is correct.)
2) Find the row of dotted lines numbered the same as the question you are answering. (Find row number 32)
3) Find the pair of dotted lines corresponding to the answer. (Find the pair of lines under the mark "B.")
4) Make a solid black mark between the dotted lines.

VI. BEFORE THE TEST

Common sense will help you find procedures to follow to get ready for an examination. Too many of us, however, overlook these sensible measures. Indeed, nervousness and fatigue have been found to be the most serious reasons why applicants fail to do their best on civil service tests. Here is a list of reminders:

- Begin your preparation early – Don't wait until the last minute to go scurrying around for books and materials or to find out what the position is all about.
- Prepare continuously – An hour a night for a week is better than an all-night cram session. This has been definitely established. What is more, a night a week for a month will return better dividends than crowding your study into a shorter period of time.
- Locate the place of the exam – You have been sent a notice telling you when and where to report for the examination. If the location is in a different town or otherwise unfamiliar to you, it would be well to inquire the best route and learn something about the building.
- Relax the night before the test – Allow your mind to rest. Do not study at all that night. Plan some mild recreation or diversion; then go to bed early and get a good night's sleep.
- Get up early enough to make a leisurely trip to the place for the test – This way unforeseen events, traffic snarls, unfamiliar buildings, etc. will not upset you.
- Dress comfortably – A written test is not a fashion show. You will be known by number and not by name, so wear something comfortable.

- Leave excess paraphernalia at home – Shopping bags and odd bundles will get in your way. You need bring only the items mentioned in the official notice you received; usually everything you need is provided. Do not bring reference books to the exam. They will only confuse those last minutes and be taken away from you when in the test room.
- Arrive somewhat ahead of time – If because of transportation schedules you must get there very early, bring a newspaper or magazine to take your mind off yourself while waiting.
- Locate the examination room – When you have found the proper room, you will be directed to the seat or part of the room where you will sit. Sometimes you are given a sheet of instructions to read while you are waiting. Do not fill out any forms until you are told to do so; just read them and be prepared.
- Relax and prepare to listen to the instructions
- If you have any physical problem that may keep you from doing your best, be sure to tell the test administrator. If you are sick or in poor health, you really cannot do your best on the exam. You can come back and take the test some other time.

VII. AT THE TEST

The day of the test is here and you have the test booklet in your hand. The temptation to get going is very strong. Caution! There is more to success than knowing the right answers. You must know how to identify your papers and understand variations in the type of short-answer question used in this particular examination. Follow these suggestions for maximum results from your efforts:

1) Cooperate with the monitor

The test administrator has a duty to create a situation in which you can be as much at ease as possible. He will give instructions, tell you when to begin, check to see that you are marking your answer sheet correctly, and so on. He is not there to guard you, although he will see that your competitors do not take unfair advantage. He wants to help you do your best.

2) Listen to all instructions

Don't jump the gun! Wait until you understand all directions. In most civil service tests you get more time than you need to answer the questions. So don't be in a hurry. Read each word of instructions until you clearly understand the meaning. Study the examples, listen to all announcements and follow directions. Ask questions if you do not understand what to do.

3) Identify your papers

Civil service exams are usually identified by number only. You will be assigned a number; you must not put your name on your test papers. Be sure to copy your number correctly. Since more than one exam may be given, copy your exact examination title.

4) Plan your time

Unless you are told that a test is a "speed" or "rate of work" test, speed itself is usually not important. Time enough to answer all the questions will be provided, but this does not mean that you have all day. An overall time limit has been set. Divide the total time (in minutes) by the number of questions to determine the approximate time you have for each question.

5) Do not linger over difficult questions

If you come across a difficult question, mark it with a paper clip (useful to have along) and come back to it when you have been through the booklet. One caution if you do this – be sure to skip a number on your answer sheet as well. Check often to be sure that you have not lost your place and that you are marking in the row numbered the same as the question you are answering.

6) Read the questions

Be sure you know what the question asks! Many capable people are unsuccessful because they failed to *read* the questions correctly.

7) Answer all questions

Unless you have been instructed that a penalty will be deducted for incorrect answers, it is better to guess than to omit a question.

8) Speed tests

It is often better NOT to guess on speed tests. It has been found that on timed tests people are tempted to spend the last few seconds before time is called in marking answers at random – without even reading them – in the hope of picking up a few extra points. To discourage this practice, the instructions may warn you that your score will be "corrected" for guessing. That is, a penalty will be applied. The incorrect answers will be deducted from the correct ones, or some other penalty formula will be used.

9) Review your answers

If you finish before time is called, go back to the questions you guessed or omitted to give them further thought. Review other answers if you have time.

10) Return your test materials

If you are ready to leave before others have finished or time is called, take ALL your materials to the monitor and leave quietly. Never take any test material with you. The monitor can discover whose papers are not complete, and taking a test booklet may be grounds for disqualification.

VIII. EXAMINATION TECHNIQUES

1) Read the general instructions carefully. These are usually printed on the first page of the exam booklet. As a rule, these instructions refer to the timing of the examination; the fact that you should not start work until the signal and must stop work at a signal, etc. If there are any *special* instructions, such as a choice of questions to be answered, make sure that you note this instruction carefully.

2) When you are ready to start work on the examination, that is as soon as the signal has been given, read the instructions to each question booklet, underline any key words or phrases, such as *least, best, outline, describe* and the like. In this way you will tend to answer as requested rather than discover on reviewing your paper that you *listed without describing*, that you selected the *worst* choice rather than the *best* choice, etc.

3) If the examination is of the objective or multiple-choice type – that is, each question will also give a series of possible answers: A, B, C or D, and you are called upon to select the best answer and write the letter next to that answer on your answer paper – it is advisable to start answering each question in turn. There may be anywhere from 50 to 100 such questions in the three or four hours allotted and you can see how much time would be taken if you read through all the questions before beginning to answer any. Furthermore, if you come across a question or group of questions which you know would be difficult to answer, it would undoubtedly affect your handling of all the other questions.

4) If the examination is of the essay type and contains but a few questions, it is a moot point as to whether you should read all the questions before starting to answer any one. Of course, if you are given a choice – say five out of seven and the like – then it is essential to read all the questions so you can eliminate the two that are most difficult. If, however, you are asked to answer all the questions, there may be danger in trying to answer the easiest one first because you may find that you will spend too much time on it. The best technique is to answer the first question, then proceed to the second, etc.

5) Time your answers. Before the exam begins, write down the time it started, then add the time allowed for the examination and write down the time it must be completed, then divide the time available somewhat as follows:
   - If 3-1/2 hours are allowed, that would be 210 minutes. If you have 80 objective-type questions, that would be an average of 2-1/2 minutes per question. Allow yourself no more than 2 minutes per question, or a total of 160 minutes, which will permit about 50 minutes to review.
   - If for the time allotment of 210 minutes there are 7 essay questions to answer, that would average about 30 minutes a question. Give yourself only 25 minutes per question so that you have about 35 minutes to review.

6) The most important instruction is to *read each question* and make sure you know what is wanted. The second most important instruction is to *time yourself properly* so that you answer every question. The third most important instruction is to *answer every question*. Guess if you have to but include something for each question. Remember that you will receive no credit for a blank and will probably receive some credit if you write something in answer to an essay question. If you guess a letter – say "B" for a multiple-choice question – you may have guessed right. If you leave a blank as an answer to a multiple-choice question, the examiners may respect your feelings but it will not add a point to your score. Some exams may penalize you for wrong answers, so in such cases *only*, you may not want to guess unless you have some basis for your answer.

7) Suggestions
   a. Objective-type questions
      1. Examine the question booklet for proper sequence of pages and questions
      2. Read all instructions carefully
      3. Skip any question which seems too difficult; return to it after all other questions have been answered
      4. Apportion your time properly; do not spend too much time on any single question or group of questions

5. Note and underline key words – *all, most, fewest, least, best, worst, same, opposite,* etc.
6. Pay particular attention to negatives
7. Note unusual option, e.g., unduly long, short, complex, different or similar in content to the body of the question
8. Observe the use of "hedging" words – *probably, may, most likely,* etc.
9. Make sure that your answer is put next to the same number as the question
10. Do not second-guess unless you have good reason to believe the second answer is definitely more correct
11. Cross out original answer if you decide another answer is more accurate; do not erase until you are ready to hand your paper in
12. Answer all questions; guess unless instructed otherwise
13. Leave time for review

b. Essay questions
   1. Read each question carefully
   2. Determine exactly what is wanted. Underline key words or phrases.
   3. Decide on outline or paragraph answer
   4. Include many different points and elements unless asked to develop any one or two points or elements
   5. Show impartiality by giving pros and cons unless directed to select one side only
   6. Make and write down any assumptions you find necessary to answer the questions
   7. Watch your English, grammar, punctuation and choice of words
   8. Time your answers; don't crowd material

8) Answering the essay question

Most essay questions can be answered by framing the specific response around several key words or ideas. Here are a few such key words or ideas:

M's: manpower, materials, methods, money, management
P's: purpose, program, policy, plan, procedure, practice, problems, pitfalls, personnel, public relations

a. Six basic steps in handling problems:
   1. Preliminary plan and background development
   2. Collect information, data and facts
   3. Analyze and interpret information, data and facts
   4. Analyze and develop solutions as well as make recommendations
   5. Prepare report and sell recommendations
   6. Install recommendations and follow up effectiveness

b. Pitfalls to avoid
   1. *Taking things for granted* – A statement of the situation does not necessarily imply that each of the elements is necessarily true; for example, a complaint may be invalid and biased so that all that can be taken for granted is that a complaint has been registered

2. *Considering only one side of a situation* – Wherever possible, indicate several alternatives and then point out the reasons you selected the best one
3. *Failing to indicate follow up* – Whenever your answer indicates action on your part, make certain that you will take proper follow-up action to see how successful your recommendations, procedures or actions turn out to be
4. *Taking too long in answering any single question* – Remember to time your answers properly

IX. AFTER THE TEST

Scoring procedures differ in detail among civil service jurisdictions although the general principles are the same. Whether the papers are hand-scored or graded by machine we have described, they are nearly always graded by number. That is, the person who marks the paper knows only the number – never the name – of the applicant. Not until all the papers have been graded will they be matched with names. If other tests, such as training and experience or oral interview ratings have been given, scores will be combined. Different parts of the examination usually have different weights. For example, the written test might count 60 percent of the final grade, and a rating of training and experience 40 percent. In many jurisdictions, veterans will have a certain number of points added to their grades.

After the final grade has been determined, the names are placed in grade order and an eligible list is established. There are various methods for resolving ties between those who get the same final grade – probably the most common is to place first the name of the person whose application was received first. Job offers are made from the eligible list in the order the names appear on it. You will be notified of your grade and your rank as soon as all these computations have been made. This will be done as rapidly as possible.

People who are found to meet the requirements in the announcement are called "eligibles." Their names are put on a list of eligible candidates. An eligible's chances of getting a job depend on how high he stands on this list and how fast agencies are filling jobs from the list.

When a job is to be filled from a list of eligibles, the agency asks for the names of people on the list of eligibles for that job. When the civil service commission receives this request, it sends to the agency the names of the three people highest on this list. Or, if the job to be filled has specialized requirements, the office sends the agency the names of the top three persons who meet these requirements from the general list.

The appointing officer makes a choice from among the three people whose names were sent to him. If the selected person accepts the appointment, the names of the others are put back on the list to be considered for future openings.

That is the rule in hiring from all kinds of eligible lists, whether they are for typist, carpenter, chemist, or something else. For every vacancy, the appointing officer has his choice of any one of the top three eligibles on the list. This explains why the person whose name is on top of the list sometimes does not get an appointment when some of the persons lower on the list do. If the appointing officer chooses the second or third eligible, the No. 1 eligible does not get a job at once, but stays on the list until he is appointed or the list is terminated.

X. HOW TO PASS THE INTERVIEW TEST

The examination for which you applied requires an oral interview test. You have already taken the written test and you are now being called for the interview test – the final part of the formal examination.

You may think that it is not possible to prepare for an interview test and that there are no procedures to follow during an interview. Our purpose is to point out some things you can do in advance that will help you and some good rules to follow and pitfalls to avoid while you are being interviewed.

What is an interview supposed to test?

The written examination is designed to test the technical knowledge and competence of the candidate; the oral is designed to evaluate intangible qualities, not readily measured otherwise, and to establish a list showing the relative fitness of each candidate – as measured against his competitors – for the position sought. Scoring is not on the basis of "right" and "wrong," but on a sliding scale of values ranging from "not passable" to "outstanding." As a matter of fact, it is possible to achieve a relatively low score without a single "incorrect" answer because of evident weakness in the qualities being measured.

Occasionally, an examination may consist entirely of an oral test – either an individual or a group oral. In such cases, information is sought concerning the technical knowledges and abilities of the candidate, since there has been no written examination for this purpose. More commonly, however, an oral test is used to supplement a written examination.

Who conducts interviews?

The composition of oral boards varies among different jurisdictions. In nearly all, a representative of the personnel department serves as chairman. One of the members of the board may be a representative of the department in which the candidate would work. In some cases, "outside experts" are used, and, frequently, a businessman or some other representative of the general public is asked to serve. Labor and management or other special groups may be represented. The aim is to secure the services of experts in the appropriate field.

However the board is composed, it is a good idea (and not at all improper or unethical) to ascertain in advance of the interview who the members are and what groups they represent. When you are introduced to them, you will have some idea of their backgrounds and interests, and at least you will not stutter and stammer over their names.

What should be done before the interview?

While knowledge about the board members is useful and takes some of the surprise element out of the interview, there is other preparation which is more substantive. It *is* possible to prepare for an oral interview – in several ways:

1) Keep a copy of your application and review it carefully before the interview

This may be the only document before the oral board, and the starting point of the interview. Know what education and experience you have listed there, and the sequence and dates of all of it. Sometimes the board will ask you to review the highlights of your experience for them; you should not have to hem and haw doing it.

2) Study the class specification and the examination announcement

Usually, the oral board has one or both of these to guide them. The qualities, characteristics or knowledges required by the position sought are stated in these documents. They offer valuable clues as to the nature of the oral interview. For example, if the job involves supervisory responsibilities, the announcement will usually indicate that knowledge of modern supervisory methods and the qualifications of the candidate as a supervisor will be tested. If so, you can expect such questions, frequently in the form of a hypothetical situation which you are expected to solve. NEVER go into an oral without knowledge of the duties and responsibilities of the job you seek.

3) Think through each qualification required

Try to visualize the kind of questions you would ask if you were a board member. How well could you answer them? Try especially to appraise your own knowledge and background in each area, *measured against the job sought*, and identify any areas in which you are weak. Be critical and realistic – do not flatter yourself.

4) Do some general reading in areas in which you feel you may be weak

For example, if the job involves supervision and your past experience has NOT, some general reading in supervisory methods and practices, particularly in the field of human relations, might be useful. Do NOT study agency procedures or detailed manuals. The oral board will be testing your understanding and capacity, not your memory.

5) Get a good night's sleep and watch your general health and mental attitude

You will want a clear head at the interview. Take care of a cold or any other minor ailment, and of course, no hangovers.

What should be done on the day of the interview?

Now comes the day of the interview itself. Give yourself plenty of time to get there. Plan to arrive somewhat ahead of the scheduled time, particularly if your appointment is in the fore part of the day. If a previous candidate fails to appear, the board might be ready for you a bit early. By early afternoon an oral board is almost invariably behind schedule if there are many candidates, and you may have to wait. Take along a book or magazine to read, or your application to review, but leave any extraneous material in the waiting room when you go in for your interview. In any event, relax and compose yourself.

The matter of dress is important. The board is forming impressions about you – from your experience, your manners, your attitude, and your appearance. Give your personal appearance careful attention. Dress your best, but not your flashiest. Choose conservative, appropriate clothing, and be sure it is immaculate. This is a business interview, and your appearance should indicate that you regard it as such. Besides, being well groomed and properly dressed will help boost your confidence.

Sooner or later, someone will call your name and escort you into the interview room. *This is it.* From here on you are on your own. It is too late for any more preparation. But remember, you asked for this opportunity to prove your fitness, and you are here because your request was granted.

What happens when you go in?

The usual sequence of events will be as follows: The clerk (who is often the board stenographer) will introduce you to the chairman of the oral board, who will introduce you to the other members of the board. Acknowledge the introductions before you sit down. Do not be surprised if you find a microphone facing you or a stenotypist sitting by. Oral interviews are usually recorded in the event of an appeal or other review.

Usually the chairman of the board will open the interview by reviewing the highlights of your education and work experience from your application – primarily for the benefit of the other members of the board, as well as to get the material into the record. Do not interrupt or comment unless there is an error or significant misinterpretation; if that is the case, do not hesitate. But do not quibble about insignificant matters. Also, he will usually ask you some question about your education, experience or your present job – partly to get you to start talking and to establish the interviewing "rapport." He may start the actual questioning, or turn it over to one of the other members. Frequently, each member undertakes the questioning on a particular area, one in which he is perhaps most competent, so you can expect each member to participate in the examination. Because time is limited, you may also expect some rather abrupt switches in the direction the questioning takes, so do not be upset by it. Normally, a board member will not pursue a single line of questioning unless he discovers a particular strength or weakness.

After each member has participated, the chairman will usually ask whether any member has any further questions, then will ask you if you have anything you wish to add. Unless you are expecting this question, it may floor you. Worse, it may start you off on an extended, extemporaneous speech. The board is not usually seeking more information. The question is principally to offer you a last opportunity to present further qualifications or to indicate that you have nothing to add. So, if you feel that a significant qualification or characteristic has been overlooked, it is proper to point it out in a sentence or so. Do not compliment the board on the thoroughness of their examination – they have been sketchy, and you know it. If you wish, merely say, "No thank you, I have nothing further to add." This is a point where you can "talk yourself out" of a good impression or fail to present an important bit of information. Remember, *you close the interview yourself.*

The chairman will then say, "That is all, Mr. _____, thank you." Do not be startled; the interview is over, and quicker than you think. Thank him, gather your belongings and take your leave. Save your sigh of relief for the other side of the door.

How to put your best foot forward

Throughout this entire process, you may feel that the board individually and collectively is trying to pierce your defenses, seek out your hidden weaknesses and embarrass and confuse you. Actually, this is not true. They are obliged to make an appraisal of your qualifications for the job you are seeking, and they want to see you in your best light. Remember, they must interview all candidates and a non-cooperative candidate may become a failure in spite of their best efforts to bring out his qualifications. Here are 15 suggestions that will help you:

1) Be natural – Keep your attitude confident, not cocky

If you are not confident that you can do the job, do not expect the board to be. Do not apologize for your weaknesses, try to bring out your strong points. The board is interested in a positive, not negative, presentation. Cockiness will antagonize any board member and make him wonder if you are covering up a weakness by a false show of strength.

2) Get comfortable, but don't lounge or sprawl

Sit erectly but not stiffly. A careless posture may lead the board to conclude that you are careless in other things, or at least that you are not impressed by the importance of the occasion. Either conclusion is natural, even if incorrect. Do not fuss with your clothing, a pencil or an ashtray. Your hands may occasionally be useful to emphasize a point; do not let them become a point of distraction.

3) Do not wisecrack or make small talk

This is a serious situation, and your attitude should show that you consider it as such. Further, the time of the board is limited – they do not want to waste it, and neither should you.

4) Do not exaggerate your experience or abilities
In the first place, from information in the application or other interviews and sources, the board may know more about you than you think. Secondly, you probably will not get away with it. An experienced board is rather adept at spotting such a situation, so do not take the chance.

5) If you know a board member, do not make a point of it, yet do not hide it
Certainly you are not fooling him, and probably not the other members of the board. Do not try to take advantage of your acquaintanceship – it will probably do you little good.

6) Do not dominate the interview
Let the board do that. They will give you the clues – do not assume that you have to do all the talking. Realize that the board has a number of questions to ask you, and do not try to take up all the interview time by showing off your extensive knowledge of the answer to the first one.

7) Be attentive
You only have 20 minutes or so, and you should keep your attention at its sharpest throughout. When a member is addressing a problem or question to you, give him your undivided attention. Address your reply principally to him, but do not exclude the other board members.

8) Do not interrupt
A board member may be stating a problem for you to analyze. He will ask you a question when the time comes. Let him state the problem, and wait for the question.

9) Make sure you understand the question
Do not try to answer until you are sure what the question is. If it is not clear, restate it in your own words or ask the board member to clarify it for you. However, do not haggle about minor elements.

10) Reply promptly but not hastily
A common entry on oral board rating sheets is "candidate responded readily," or "candidate hesitated in replies." Respond as promptly and quickly as you can, but do not jump to a hasty, ill-considered answer.

11) Do not be peremptory in your answers
A brief answer is proper – but do not fire your answer back. That is a losing game from your point of view. The board member can probably ask questions much faster than you can answer them.

12) Do not try to create the answer you think the board member wants
He is interested in what kind of mind you have and how it works – not in playing games. Furthermore, he can usually spot this practice and will actually grade you down on it.

13) Do not switch sides in your reply merely to agree with a board member
Frequently, a member will take a contrary position merely to draw you out and to see if you are willing and able to defend your point of view. Do not start a debate, yet do not surrender a good position. If a position is worth taking, it is worth defending.

14) Do not be afraid to admit an error in judgment if you are shown to be wrong

The board knows that you are forced to reply without any opportunity for careful consideration. Your answer may be demonstrably wrong. If so, admit it and get on with the interview.

15) Do not dwell at length on your present job

The opening question may relate to your present assignment. Answer the question but do not go into an extended discussion. You are being examined for a *new* job, not your present one. As a matter of fact, try to phrase ALL your answers in terms of the job for which you are being examined.

Basis of Rating

Probably you will forget most of these "do's" and "don'ts" when you walk into the oral interview room. Even remembering them all will not ensure you a passing grade. Perhaps you did not have the qualifications in the first place. But remembering them will help you to put your best foot forward, without treading on the toes of the board members.

Rumor and popular opinion to the contrary notwithstanding, an oral board wants you to make the best appearance possible. They know you are under pressure – but they also want to see how you respond to it as a guide to what your reaction would be under the pressures of the job you seek. They will be influenced by the degree of poise you display, the personal traits you show and the manner in which you respond.

ABOUT THIS BOOK

This book contains tests divided into Examination Sections. Go through each test, answering every question in the margin. We have also attached a sample answer sheet at the back of the book that can be removed and used. At the end of each test look at the answer key and check your answers. On the ones you got wrong, look at the right answer choice and learn. Do not fill in the answers first. Do not memorize the questions and answers, but understand the answer and principles involved. On your test, the questions will likely be different from the samples. Questions are changed and new ones added. If you understand these past questions you should have success with any changes that arise. Tests may consist of several types of questions. We have additional books on each subject should more study be advisable or necessary for you. Finally, the more you study, the better prepared you will be. This book is intended to be the last thing you study before you walk into the examination room. Prior study of relevant texts is also recommended. NLC publishes some of these in our Fundamental Series. Knowledge and good sense are important factors in passing your exam. Good luck also helps. So now study this Passbook, absorb the material contained within and take that knowledge into the examination. Then do your best to pass that exam.

EXAMINATION SECTION

EXAMINATION SECTION
TEST 1

DIRECTIONS: Each question or incomplete statement is followed by several suggested answers or completions. Select the one that BEST answers the question or completes the statement. *PRINT THE LETTER OF THE CORRECT ANSWER IN THE SPACE AT THE RIGHT.*

1. Which of the following is a behavior that can impact customer service?　　　　1.____
   A. Greeting customers promptly
   B. Believing in a positive mission statement
   C. Giving great service
   D. Poor work attitude

2. What are vital behaviors?　　　　2.____
   A. Ones that are mandated by law
   B. Specific actions that have the maximum impact on customer service
   C. Of no particular importance when influencing employees
   D. The same as good attitudes

3. Of the following, the MOST effective icebreaker when greeting a customer would be:　　　　3.____
   A. Talking about local interests such as a sports team or the weather
   B. Expression appreciation for the customer visiting you today
   C. Finding out and expressing interest in something the customer shows interest in
   D. All of the above

4. Which of the following actions would get customers to interact with you and, therefore, the organization you represent?　　　　4.____
   A. Inviting the customers to fill out paperwork
   B. Help the customer sample the company's culture
   C. Both A and B
   D. None of the above

5. Of the following options, the BIGGEST issue with not greeting a customer promptly is:　　　　5.____
   A. The customer might not leave as quickly as you'd like them to
   B. The organization misses an opportunity to establish a positive relationship
   C. They may estimate that their wait was shorter than it actually was
   D. Both A and C

6. Which of the following actions is it important to take when someone makes an oral presentation to a large group of customers?　　　　6.____
   A. Relax the audience by moving back and forth when speaking
   B. Avoid eye contact with anyone in the audience
   C. Speak loudly enough for all to hear your message
   D. Turn your back to the audience when presenting visual aids

1

7. Of the following techniques for writing effective communication (i.e., business letters) to customers, which of the following helps a person be consistently on message the MOST?
   A. Preparing outlines
   B. Development and inclusion of charts
   C. Consulting references
   D. Asking questions

   7.____

8. Persuasive messages that ask a person to do something should be communicated in a way that makes it easy for that person to
   A. plan accordingly
   B. answer politely
   C. organize logically
   D. respond positively

   8.____

9. If an organization wishes to emphasize customer service skills such as courtesy and friendliness, when should said organization focus on these skills?
   A. When designing their facilities
   B. During market research
   C. When meeting for technology planning
   D. During the hiring process

   9.____

10. If an organization realizes they need to improve their technology to better meet customer demands and desires, this would have to result from a business activity known as
    A. continuity improvement
    B. business process management
    C. employee training and in-service
    D. organizational positioning

    10.____

11. When in the distribution channel business, what is an important thing to keep in mind concerning customers?
    A. Most expect low service levels.
    B. Many want immediate delivery.
    C. Everyone defines service differently.
    D. A number of customers tend to refuse late shipments.

    11.____

12. When persuading a customer to go along with a proposed change from their initial query, you should
    A. explain how the change will benefit them
    B. tell them you have a better way of doing things
    C. minimize the amount of information you share with them
    D. reinforce your ideas with facts and statistics

    12.____

13. Which of the following statements regarding using the internet to administer questionnaires is TRUE?
    A. Interviewers are more likely to influence respondents' answers online.
    B. Online questionnaires require more time for data entry and collection.
    C. Respondents are more likely to misunderstand online questionnaires.
    D. Data entry and administrative costs are higher for online questionnaires.

    13.____

14. After a series of governmental scandals, a public service organization wants the public to perceive it as more trustworthy and embarks on an advertising campaign to aid the makeover. What goal does this illustrate?
    A. Projecting a certain image
    B. Achieving stability
    C. Increasing customer service and productivity
    D. All of the above

15. When presenting information to a small group of customers, you decided to use presentation software to prepare your multimedia presentation. What is the purpose of using this software?
    A. To develop websites
    B. To maintain customer files
    C. To access online resources
    D. To support your report findings

16. A current trend in hospitality of customers is to build loyal customer relationships and enhance service levels by optimizing the use of
    A. independent agents
    B. internet web sites
    C. satellite roving devices
    D. service rating advisors

17. Which of the following would be an excellent example of an employee empathizing with a customer's objection?
    A. "I understand how you feel."
    B. "You must think the price is too high."
    C. "Everyone knows this is how this process works."
    D. "I really don't see what you don't understand about this."

18. Customer service experts who use the services and products they are in charge of dispensing are able to suggest appropriate substitute services and products because of their own personal
    A. preference
    B. feelings
    C. experience
    D. opinion

19. An employee should always attempt to answer a customer's questions thoroughly and explain the benefits of the service so that the customer will
    A. make a quicker decision
    B. be in a state of indecision
    C. think about making a decision
    D. feel better about the purchasing decision

20. One should be able to adjust his customer service style from one customer to another so that he can appeal to each customer's
    A. natural aptitude
    B. unique personality
    C. hidden objection
    D. internal ability

21. In order to attract customers and encourage them to visit the facilities, what do many organizations do?
    A. Market trips
    B. Trade shows
    C. Press kits
    D. Special events

22. What kind of question is a person asking if they ask the following: "What level of service would you like today?"   22.____
    A. Interpretive   B. Impersonal
    C. Open-ended   D. Assumptive

23. Your organization holds a meeting to identify community issues with which they can involve themselves.   23.____
    Which of the following options should the organization consider when deciding which community issue to involve themselves with?
    It should
    A. contribute to the social good   B. earn a reasonable profit
    C. boost employee loyalty   D. support controversial topics

24. If a person's thoughts, emotions, and physical sensations interfere with their listening skills, that is referred to as   24.____
    A. cultural diversity   B. internal noise
    C. cultural norms   D. external noise

25. Which of the following is NOT a characteristic of information literacy?   25.____
    The ability to
    A. use information to manipulate others
    B. determine what information is needed for a presentation
    C. find information relevant to a topic
    D. use information to create new knowledge

KEY (CORRECT ANSWERS)

1. A
2. B
3. D
4. C
5. B

6. C
7. A
8. D
9. D
10. B

11. C
12. A
13. C
14. A
15. D

16. B
17. A
18. C
19. D
20. B

21. D
22. C
23. A
24. B
25. A

TEST 2

DIRECTIONS: Each question or incomplete statement is followed by several suggested answers or completions. Select the one that BEST answers the question or completes the statement. *PRINT THE LETTER OF THE CORRECT ANSWER IN THE SPACE AT THE RIGHT.*

1. When preparing to deliver a speech, what is the purpose of writing key points on notecards and then placing those cards in order of their importance?
    A. To verify their authenticity
    B. To access files
    C. To revise facts
    D. To organize information

    1.____

2. An employee who is originally from Ecuador meets with a client from London, England and when the employee attempts to shake the client's hand, the client backs away.
   What cultural issue should the employee be aware of next time to avoid this misstep?
    A. Punctuality
    B. Personal space preferences
    C. Appearance
    D. Language variances

    2.____

3. An employee who demonstrates self-confidence has which of the following characteristics?
    A. They take few risks because they fear making mistakes.
    B. They exhibit aggressive behavior when expressing their opinion.
    C. They realize that mistakes are a part of personal growth.
    D. They are overly concerned with what others say about them.

    3.____

4. An employee is working with a client for an hour going over the features of a service they offer when the client interrupts and says, "I can find this service for a lot less than what you are offer. Your price is preposterous!"
   If the employee wishes to reply in the most professional manner as possible, they would do which of the following?
    A. Attempt to explain the benefits of the service from this organization over another.
    B. Stop helping the client and begin to find someone else to help.
    C. Ask a supervisor to help convince the client to purchase the service there.
    D. Thank the client politely for coming in today.

    4.____

5. You are working with a customer who asks you questions about aspects of the organization that you are clearly not familiar with. A coworker overhears the conversation and offers to help.
   What is the FIRST thing you should do?
    A. Politely refuse the help and attempt to answer the customer's questions anyway.
    B. Accept the offer of help and listen to the answers the coworker gives to the customer.
    C. Ignore the coworker. They only want to look good in front of your supervisor.
    D. Let the other associate take over and look for a new customer to help.

    5.____

6. A customer comes up to an employee with a broken item from the store. They say they bought the item a month ago and now it does not work. What is the FIRST thing the employee should do?
    A. "With this kind of item, it's best you check simple things like the batteries first. I will check for you."
    B. "We've never had anyone return this item before. What did you or your child do to it?"
    C. "Are you sure you bought this item at our store? Do you have your receipt?"
    D. "We've had a lot of issues with that item. You should probably contact the manufacturer."

6.____

7. When a person first encounters an employee and forms a lasting mental image of that employee and, therefore, the organization, that is called
    A. attitude impact
    B. self-confidence
    C. first impression
    D. workplace ethics

7.____

8. Which of the following convey to clients that a person is professional?
    A. No wrinkles, creases or stains
    B. No large, loud prints
    C. Well-tailored, formal clothing
    D. All of the above

8.____

9. An employee is put in charge of email communications for the organization and asks you for help.
   Which of the following would NOT be considered good email etiquette?
    A. Keeping emails brief and to the point
    B. Putting the purpose of the email in the subject field
    C. Sending humorous YouTube videos and personal emails to customers
    D. Using a signature that includes contact information that follows your message

9.____

10. An employee is holding a meeting for clients and is just about to conclude when another client shows up late.
    Which of the following actions would be the BEST to take?
    A. Thank the client for stopping by and pause the meeting momentarily to fill the client in on what they missed.
    B. Once the meeting is over, remind the client that punctuality is incredibly important to your organization. Then once they seem to understand the importance of being on time, fill them in on what they missed.
    C. Openly criticize the client in front of everyone else for being tardy. Once you've criticized them, fill them in on what they missed.
    D. Slightly nod to the client when they enter, but continue the meeting without bringing them up to speed. Once the meeting concludes, fill the client in if the wish to be brought up to speed.

10.____

11. You are running 15 minutes late to a meeting with a client. 11._____
    What should you do?
    A. Call the client and tell them you will be there in a few minutes.
    B. The client won't mind waiting. Fifteen minutes is not that long of a wait.
    C. Have your coworker talk to the client and tell them you were involved in a minor traffic accident that is causing you to be delayed.
    D. Pretend like you thought the meeting was supposed to be on a different day. Send an email apologizing for the inconvenience.

12. A longtime friend has stopped at your work to visit you before they fly home. 12._____
    You are currently working with customers when he shows up.
    What should you do?
    A. Have your friend join the meeting and introduce him to your customers.
    B. Tell your friend to wait in the break room/cafeteria and meet him when you finish up your meeting with the customers.
    C. Stop the meeting immediately and tell the customers to reschedule with you tomorrow. You also let them know they will have priority in terms of meeting times.
    D. Speed through the rest of the meeting and do not stop to ask if anyone has any questions. Then find your friend afterwards.

13. A coworker is currently working with customers when you notice your favorite 13._____
    song starts playing from your computer. You
    A. dance around the office after blasting the music on your speakers
    B. listen to the music with your headphones at a loud volume so that the customers can hear a muted version of the song
    C. listen to the music with your headphones in at a low volume so that you do not disturb others and are still accessible in case coworkers/customers need you
    D. listen to your music with noise-cancelling headphones, so that you cannot hear others if they request your attention

14. You have an important meeting with customers and they will be meeting you 14._____
    around dinner time.
    Where should you bring them for the dinner meeting?
    A. Ask them their preference for food and pick the corresponding restaurant.
    B. An upscale French restaurant known for its romantic ambience
    C. A sports bar that will be airing an important playoff game
    D. Order Chinese food and invite them to the office

15. An employee has an important presentation in front of customers today, but it 15._____
    is also "Casual Friday."
    How should the employee dress? Why?
    A. Dress casually. The customers will understand that Casual Fridays are for casual dress, so they will not be upset.
    B. Business casual. An employee wants to assure customers that they handle business the way they dress, which means a smart, but comfortable look.

C. A little nicer than normally, but nothing too formal. This way they are still comfortable, but the customer knows that they are important too.
D. Dress in pajamas. Customers do not care what an employee wears as long as their presentation is good.

16. Professionally, what is the longest it should take someone to respond to a client email? How about a phone call? 16._____
    A. 45 minutes; 15 minutes
    B. 24 hours; 24 hours
    C. 48 hours; 24 hours
    D. 24 hours; 4 hours

17. Unlike social etiquette, office and business professionalism are PRIMARILY based on 17._____
    A. hierarchy and power
    B. personal relations between employees and customers
    C. common sense and courtesy
    D. both A and C

18. If something goes wrong during a customer interaction or presentation, what should you do? 18._____
    A. Clear your head, focus, and be cheerful and professional and act like nothing went wrong
    B. Take responsibility and take appropriate action
    C. Blame others for your technical difficulties
    D. Find a way to end the interaction as quickly as possible

19. What is the ultimate goal of customer service? 19._____
    A. Customer satisfaction
    B. Understanding customers
    C. Identify problems
    D. Improve product and service

20. Of the following, which is the BEST reason for employees and supervisors to frequently gauge customer satisfaction? 20._____
    A. No reason. One evaluation is enough.
    B. Because employees are not always honest about reporting customer satisfaction.
    C. They may have concerns or complaints that they have not voiced.
    D. Complaints do not always reach management.

21. Which of the following is TRUE of scope of influence? 21._____
    A. It is objective.
    B. Some have a larger scope of influence than others.
    C. Everyone has the same scope of influence.
    D. It is not relevant to customer service.

22. Which of the following techniques will create credibility in the minds of customers? 22._____
    A. Never admit being wrong. It undermines credibility.
    B. Demonstrate your human emotions. Whether you're angry or happy, let others see it.

C. Tell people what they want to hear even if it is not necessarily what you know to be true.
D. Become an expert about various factors in your profession. People will respect your knowledge.

23. You are in a "train the trainer" meeting about meeting customer expectations. As you talk in small groups after a short presentation, four people express very different statements about customer expectations.
Which one is CORRECT?
    A. "Wrong. Customer expectations are always changing."
    B. "Customer expectations rarely change."
    C. "Guys, all you really have to do is make a promise to solve customer problems. They forget after a while, even if you don't follow through."
    D. "Do not worry about what other companies are doing. We should focus on ourselves."

23.____

24. Of the following, which of the following is TRUE concerning customer service?
    A. Average customer service will always suffice.
    B. Customers lost through poor customer service are easy to replace.
    C. Organizations must provide excellent customer service or expect failure.
    D. None of the above

24.____

25. You are in a situation with a challenging customer.
How should you handle this situation?
    A. Make them respect and value your time.
    B. Avoid admitting any wrongdoing on your part.
    C. Find a solution and implement it.
    D. Do not show empathy.

25.____

KEY (CORRECT ANSWERS)

1. D
2. B
3. C
4. A
5. B

6. A
7. C
8. D
9. C
10. D

11. A
12. B
13. C
14. A
15. B

16. D
17. D
18. B
19. A
20. C

21. B
22. D
23. A
24. C
25. C

EXAMINATION SECTION
TEST 1

DIRECTIONS: Each question or incomplete statement is followed by several suggested answers or completions. Select the one that BEST answers the question or completes the statement. *PRINT THE LETTER OF THE CORRECT ANSWER IN THE SPACE AT THE RIGHT.*

1. A woman in her mid-30s comes up to your desk and asks you how she can apply to work at your office. You do not know the immediate answer to that question.
   Which of the following would be the BEST way to respond to her request?
   A. Tell her what sounds like the right answer
   B. Tell her to talk to your boss and show her how to do that
   C. Explain you are not allowed to give out confidential information to the public
   D. Inform her that you do not know right now, but you will find out

2. A person approaches the customer service desk and asks you to do something that you are ultimately unable to do.
   Which of the following should you avoid doing next?
   A. Opening your policy handbook and reading from it verbatim
   B. Clarifying why you cannot do what he or she is asking of you
   C. Crafting detailed and precise statements
   D. Giving the person alternative options

3. When talking to someone from the public, which of the following statements would be LEAST frustrating for the customer to hear?
   A. "You'll have to…" B. "Mr. X will be back at any moment…"
   C. "Let me see what I can do…" D. "I'll do my best…"

4. Your office recently received a letter from an individual expressing extreme frustration and disappointment at how it was handling the customer's problems. You have written an apology letter and are reviewing it before sending it to the customer.
   You should ensure the letter is NOT
   A. sincere B. official
   C. personal D. sent immediately

5. If you are unable to provide a certain service or product with dependability and accuracy, it would be defined as a lack of
   A. courtesy B. reliability C. assurance D. responsiveness

6. As most civil service employees know, customer feedback can be, and usually is, an integral part of customer service.
   Which of the following feedback scenarios would be MOST useful to your organization?
   A. When it is an ongoing feedback system
   B. When centered on internal customers
   C. When it is focused on only a few indicators
   D. When every employee can see the feedback coming in

7. Which of the following is the LEAST important factor in making sure a customer survey is a valuable tool for your company?
   A. Taking every precaution to ensure the survey input is maintained in a confidential manner
   B. Making sure the customers believe in the confidentiality of the survey
   C. Ensuring confidentiality by having an outside company administer the survey
   D. Making sure the employees buy in and promote the survey to customers

8. Which of the following would NOT be considered part of the resolution process when identifying and dealing with a customers' problems?
   A. Following up with the customer after resolving the issue
   B. Listening and responding to each complaint the customer registers
   C. Giving the customer what they originally requested
   D. Promising the customer whatever you need to

9. A customer approaches you with a complaint. You want to arrive at a fair solution to the problem.
   What is the FIRST step you should take in this situation?
   A. Immediately defend your company from any customer criticisms
   B. Listen to the customer describe their problem
   C. Ask the customer questions to confirm the type of problem they are having
   D. Determine a solution to the customer's problem(s)

10. If you are dealing with a customer in a prompt manner when addressing their complaints or issues, which of the following are you demonstrating?
    A. Assurance   B. Empathy
    C. Responsiveness   D. Reliability

11. Steve has recently been hired to work at the postal office in town. A customer comes into the office to complain about the number of packages of his they have lost over the past year.
    When Steve attempts to help the upset customer, what should he make sure to do FIRST?
    He should
    A. check into how legitimate the customer's complaints are and see if he can do anything about the missing packages
    B. just let the customer blow off some steam and chalk it up to an emotional outburst

C. ask for help from his boss to see how to handle the situation
D. assume the complaints are accurate and immediately attempt to correct them

12. How should a service representative react when a customer first presents them with a request?
    A. Apologize
    B. Greet them in a friendly manner
    C. Read from the employee handbook about the request
    D. Ask the customer to clarify information

13. In order to assuage a customer's frustration, which of the following should a civil service employee demonstrate?
    A. Compassion   B. Indifference   C. Surprise   D. Agreement

14. A customer comes into the office requesting that your organization do something for them that you know is not part of organization policy.
    Your FIRST responsibility would be to
    A. pass the customer on to higher management to deal with the issue
    B. persuade the customer to believe that the organization can grant their request
    C. mold expectations so they more closely resemble what the organization can do for the customer
    D. tell the customer there is no way you can comply with their request

15. Of the following potential distractors, which one MOST prevents a civil service employee from displaying good listening skills while a customer is speaking?
    A. Cell phones or checking e-mail
    B. Asking superfluous questions
    C. Background office noise
    D. Interrupting the customer to speak with colleagues

16. If you are in a situation where you have to deliver a negative response to a customer, it is often better to say _____ instead of just saying "no"?
    A. "I will try to…"   B. "You can…"
    C. "Our policy does not allow…"   D. "I do not believe…"

17. You are working one-on-one with a customer.
    Which of the following would be the MOST appropriate body language to display?
    A. Make frowning faces
    B. Stare at a spot over the customer's shoulder
    C. Lean in toward the customer
    D. Cross your arms while they speak

18. The majority of communication in face-to-face meetings with customers is shown through
    A. word choice   B. tone
    C. clothing choice   D. body language

19. A customer angrily approaches you at your service desk and starts expressing his frustration with recent actions by your department.
    Which of the following should be your FIRST responses to the customer?
    A. Listen to the person, then express understanding and apologize for how they have been negatively affected by your department's action
    B. Interrupt them while they are speaking and tell them to calm down or you will not help them
    C. Give them an explanation of why your department took the actions they did
    D. None of the above

20. Of the following services, which one is NOT customized to a specific individual's needs?
    A. Hair salon
    B. Elementary education
    C. Computer counseling
    D. Dental care

21. Which of the following civil service employees demonstrates excellent customer service?
    A. A park ranger who minimizes public interaction and contact
    B. The Postal Service employee who sees the customer as a commodity
    C. The office clerk who spends a lot of time with customers sharing personal stories and anecdotes
    D. A DMV employee with open body language and direct communication

22. It is important to have excellent knowledge of services and products, if applicable, when interacting with consumers because
    A. you can demonstrate your knowledge and impress the customer
    B. your organization can have a higher margin of profit regardless of customer benefit
    C. the customer's needs can best be matched with appropriate services/products
    D. you can look good to your superiors and keep your job

23. A park ranger has recently been coming to a kids' camp dirty and unkempt. Even though her job requires her to be outside at ties, why should she still care about her personal appearance?
    A. To speed up her service to the public
    B. So she is seen as a professional in her field
    C. It would help her organizational skills
    D. To show her level of expertise as a park ranger

24. How could guided conversation be a positive with interacting with the public?
    A. It allows you to anticipate a person's needs and expectations.
    B. Most people know what they want even before they show up to your office.
    C. It creates the impression of friendliness.
    D. It helps time move faster.

25. In the event a conflict or crisis arises, which of the following would be considered a POOR action to take when interacting with the public?
    A. Provide a constant flow of information
    B. Put the public's needs first
    C. Avoid saying "No Comment" as much as possible
    D. Assign multiple spokespeople so media calls can be dealt with efficiently

25.____

KEY (CORRECT ANSWERS)

1.	D		11.	A
2.	A		12.	D
3.	C		13.	A
4.	B		14.	C
5.	B		15.	D
6.	A		16.	B
7.	C		17.	C
8.	D		18.	D
9.	B		19.	A
10.	C		20.	B

21. D
22. C
23. B
24. A
25. D

TEST 2

DIRECTIONS: Each question or incomplete statement is followed by several suggested answers or completions. Select the one that BEST answers the question or completes the statement. *PRINT THE LETTER OF THE CORRECT ANSWER IN THE SPACE AT THE RIGHT.*

1. John Smith answers a caller who struggles to understand a convoluted policy of your agency.
   How should he handle the customer's question?
   A. Tell the caller to go to the agency's website
   B. He should be honest and say he does not know the answer to the question
   C. John should explain the policy in general terms and refer them to a written version of the policy
   D. Tell the caller to talk to his supervisor and then give the caller the supervisor's extension

   1.____

2. While meeting with a group of young campers at the local parks and recreation office, you conduct a lecture on the importance of avoiding dangerous plants near the forest.
   What can you do to make sure your inexperienced audience remembers the main points of your presentation?
   A. Use flashy visuals that catch the eye
   B. Repeat and emphasize your points
   C. Make jokes so the presentation is livelier
   D. Allow the campers to ask questions at the end of the presentation

   2.____

3. A park ranger is about to deliver a speech at a public conservation meeting. Which of the following is the MOST important thing to keep in mind as he preps for the presentation?
   A. How large the audience is
   B. Whether or not he will be able to use visual aids
   C. If he will have time to use charts and graphs
   D. Audience interests

   3.____

4. Jerry receives a letter from a customer and is about to shred it without reading. When you stop him, he says that there is no reason to read it because you cannot learn very much from letters you receive from the public.
   Which of the following should you tell him in order to convince him that reading letters sent from the public is beneficial and necessary?
   A. These public letters can give us a feel for how we are meeting customer needs.
   B. Letters from the public tell us how well our informational efforts are working.
   C. These letters can inform us of what additional training we may need.
   D. The letters can tell us whether public information processes need to be changed or not.

   4.____

5. Ms. Johnson is a volunteer with the Parks and Recreation Department and her children also attend various summer programs through the district. She comes to you today to complain that one of her children was not allowed to join a program because they missed the sign-up by one day. She calls your staff a bunch of "morons" and complains that your department's actions are creating serious issues for her.
How should you handle this situation?
    A. Let Ms. Johnson rant until she gets it out of her system
    B. Tell her you cannot help her and will ask her to leave if she cannot stop referring to your colleagues as "morons"
    C. Refer Ms. Johnson to your boss
    D. Try to alter the tone of the conversation to a more objective and less emotional discussion of Ms. Johnson's problems

5.____

6. A civil service employee is tasked with moderating a town hall meeting regarding child safety, but he knows that residents will be attending the meeting with different motives.
How can the employee make sure the town hall meeting is as beneficial and informational as possible?
    A. Ask attendees to be open to changing their opinions and preferences
    B. Start out by recognizing the various motives but also stress the common objectives and interests
    C. Call out individuals who you know have specific reasons for attending and put them on the spot
    D. Cancel the meeting and avoid rescheduling it until you can be sure everyone is on the same page

6.____

7. During the question-and-answer session at the end of a presentation, a member of the public makes a suggestion that you deem not only practical but worthy of further discussion.
How should you react to this?
    A. Tell them you will let the appropriate people know of the suggestion
    B. Tell the person you concur with them wholeheartedly
    C. Let the person know you think it is a good idea but you cannot make decisions based on suggestions during Q and A
    D. Even though the suggestion is good, tell the person that someone in your organization has probably already thought of the idea

7.____

8. When in a conversation with a group of local residents, what is the BIGGEST problem with one or two people dominating the conversation?
    A. Your interaction could take longer than it should
    B. Some people will become distracted and not focus on the meeting anymore
    C. The other member of the group may not have an opportunity to share their opinions
    D. None of the above

8.____

9. You receive a phone call at the village hall, but the information being requested would need to come from the police station.
   How should you respond to the caller?
   A. Give them the police station's website and wish them well
   B. Tell them you are not responsible for their request
   C. Refer them to the police station's number and information
   D. Provide them with the information as best as you can

9._____

10. Which of the following should almost always be avoided when interacting with a member of the community?
    A. Contentious matters
    B. Topics about financial material
    C. Rules and regulations
    D. Technical lingo or jargon

10._____

11. When people use inflammatory language laced with obscenities, a town employee should
    A. refuse to continue the dialogue if the person cannot stop using the offensive language
    B. tell the person to talk to your supervisor
    C. allow the person to finish "venting" before attempting to find a solution to the problem
    D. hang up if on the phone; if in person, leave the area and ask the individual to leave as well

11._____

12. A member of the public has sent your agency a letter.
    Which of the following will help you figure out how much explaining you need to do when writing a response?
    A. Go to the agency website and search for how much explanation is provided there
    B. Take out the original customer letter and study it
    C. Presume the person who wrote the letter already has a working knowledge of the subject and thus will not require a lot of background explanation
    D. Look at past letters sent by your agency

12._____

13. During an informational meeting with local townspeople, a man makes a suggestion for a new town measure that is based on incorrect information and is impractical.
    What is the BEST way to handle a situation such as this?
    A. Ask if anyone else in attendance would like to respond to the suggestion
    B. Tell the person it is a great idea even though you are aware of its folly
    C. Thank the man for coming and tell everyone you always welcome their suggestions
    D. Inform the person that his/her comment clearly reflects an inferior knowledge about the subject

13._____

14. A member from the public calls your office about negative comments he has heard about one of your programs. You believe the comments were made by someone who had inaccurate material, but you are not completely certain of that because you are not directly involved with the program.

14._____

What is the BEST way to handle this situation?
- A. Tell the caller you will analyze the situation in depth and then call them back
- B. Tell the caller the evidence on which they have based their judgment is not supported
- C. Explain that your office has a "No Comment" policy regarding negative comments
- D. Let the caller know you are not involved with the program directly, and tell them to call the person who is

15. Which of the following quotes reflects the BEST way to handle an angry resident that keeps interrupting during a village meeting?
    - A. "I am here as a volunteer and I do not need this."
    - B. "I understand your anger, but we have quite a bit of information to cover tonight, so in fairness to everyone else, please let me continue."
    - C. "Every crowd has one black sheep in it."
    - D. "Sir, (or Ma'am) if you cannot stop interjecting, I will have security escort you from the premises."

16. Of the following, which is an example of nonverbal communication?
    - A. Frowning
    - B. Hand signs
    - C. A "21 Gun Salute"
    - D. All of the above

17. Residents of Masterton, Georgia, were recently made aware that the main road into and out of town will be under construction for the next four years. The construction will make travel time much more difficult for the citizens and they have demanded a meeting with your department. You are tasked with creating a presentation to explain to them why the construction is necessary.
    At the start of the presentation, you should
    - A. make a joke to lighten the mood
    - B. state the purpose of your presentation
    - C. provide a detailed account of the history behind the project
    - D. make a call to action

18. When a member of the public asks questions that are confusing or you do not understand right away, what is the BEST way to handle this situation?
    - A. Answer the question as you understand it
    - B. Stick to generalizations dealing with the subject of the question
    - C. Rephrase the question and ask the person if you understood what they were asking
    - D. Ask the person to repeat the question

19. When preparing for a public interaction, which of the following situations would be MOST appropriate to include handouts?
    - A. If you want to help the attendees remember important information after the interaction is over
    - B. If you want to keep the interaction short

C. When you want to remember key points to talk about
D. When you do not want attendees to have to pay attention during the interaction

20. John is in the process of handling a phone call when a local citizen approaches his desk to ask a question. Neither the caller nor the visitor seem to be in a crisis.
What should John do in this scenario?
    A. Keep talking with the caller until he is finished. Then tell the visitor he is sorry for making them wait.
    B. Remain on the phone with the caller but look up at the visitor every once and awhile so they know he has not forgotten about them.
    C. Tell the caller he has a visitor, so the conversation needs to end.
    D. Tell the visitor he will be with them as soon as he finishes the phone call.

21. When engaged in conversation with another person, which communication technique is MOST likely to ensure you comprehend fully what the other person to trying to communicate to you?
    A. Repeat back to the person what you think they are communicating
    B. Continual eye contact
    C. Making sure the person speaks slowly
    D. Nodding your head while they speak

22. You encounter someone who is frustrated about a situation and needs to vent by talking it out before they can move onto a productive conversation.
When a situation is like this, it is often BEST to
    A. recommend various strategies for calming down
    B. Ask to be excused from the conversation without offering why
    C. Explain to the person that it is unproductive to behave the way they are currently behaving
    D. Acknowledge that venting is a crucial step to moving past the emotions and allow the person to express his or her feelings

23. Which of the following is NOT an example of active listening?
    A. Taking notes
    B. Referring the customer to the manager after they are done speaking
    C. Using phrases like "I see" or "Go on"
    D. Repeating back to the customer what you've heard

24. Which of the following questions would be classified as a clarification question?
    A. "How long have you sold spoiled meat?"
    B. "Do you like our brand?"
    C. "You mentioned you liked this merchandise. How would you feel about this?"
    D. None of the above

25. When interacting with a member of the public, which of the following words should you avoid using as it is not positive as perceived by most people? 25.____
    A. "Absolutely"
    B. "You are welcome"
    C. "Here's what I can do"
    D. "I'll do my best"

KEY (CORRECT ANSWERS)

1.	C	11.	A
2.	B	12.	B
3.	D	13.	C
4.	A	14.	A
5.	D	15.	B
6.	B	16.	D
7.	A	17.	B
8.	C	18.	C
9.	C	19.	A
10.	D	20.	D

21. A
22. D
23. B
24. C
25. D

EXAMINATION SECTION
TEST 1

DIRECTIONS: Each question or incomplete statement is followed by several suggested answers or completions. Select the one that BEST answers the question or completes the statement. *PRINT THE LETTER OF THE CORRECT ANSWER IN THE SPACE AT THE RIGHT.*

1. Good procedure in handling complaints from the public may be divided into the following four principal stages:
   I. Investigation of the complaint
   II. Receipt of the complaint
   III. Assignment of responsibility for investigation and correction
   IV. Notification of correction

   The ORDER in which these stages ordinarily come is:
   A. III, II, I, IV   B. II, III, I, IV   C. II, III, IV, I   D. II, IV, III, I

   1.____

2. The department may expect the MOST severe public criticism if
   A. it asks for an increase in its annual budget
   B. it purchases new and costly street cleaning equipment
   C. sanitation officers and men are reclassified to higher salary grades
   D. there is delay in cleaning streets of snow

   2.____

3. The MOST important function of public relations in the department should be to
   A. develop cooperation on the part of the public in keeping streets clean
   B. get stricter penalties enacted for health code violations
   C. recruit candidates for entrance positions who ca be developed into supervisors
   D. train career personnel so that they can advance in the department

   3.____

4. The one of the following which has MOST frequently elicited unfavorable public comment has been
   A. dirty sidewalks or streets   B. dumping on lot
   C. failure to curb dogs   D. overflowing garbage cans

   4.____

5. It has been suggested that, as a public relations measure, sections hold *open house* for the public.
   The MOST effective time for this would be
   A. during the summer when children are not in school and can accompany their parents
   B. during the winter when show is likely to fall and the public can see snow removal preparations
   C. immediately after a heavy snow storm when department snow removal operations are in full progress
   D. when street sanitation is receiving general attention as during *Keep City Clean* week

   5.____

25

6. When a public agency conducts a public relations program, it is MOST likely to find that each recipient of its message will
   A. disagree with the basic purpose of the message if the officials are not well known to him
   B. accept the message if it is presented by someone perceived as having a definite intention to persuade
   C. ignore the message unless it is presented in a literate and clever manner
   D. give greater attention to certain portions of the message as a result of his individual and cultural differences

7. Following are three statements about public relations and communications:
   I. A person who seeks to influence public opinion can speed up a trend
   II. Mass communications is the exposure of a mass audience to an idea
   III. All media are equally effective in reaching opinion leaders
   Which of the following choices CORRECTLY classifies the above statements into those which are correct and those which are not?
   A. I and II are correct, but III is not.
   B. II and III are correct, but I is not.
   C. I and III are correct, but II is not.
   D. III is correct, but I and II are not.

8. Public relations experts say that MAXIMUM effect for a message results from
   A. concentrating in one medium
   B. ignoring mass media and concentrating on *opinion makers*
   C. presenting only those factors which support a given position
   D. using a combination of two or more of the available media

9. To assure credibility and avoid hostility, the public relations man MUST
   A. make certain his message is truthful, not evasive or exaggerated
   B. make sure his message contains some dire consequence if ignored
   C. repeat the message often enough so that it cannot be ignored
   D. try to reach as many people and groups as possible

10. The public relations man MUST be prepared to assume that members of his audience
    A. may have developed attitudes toward his proposals—favorable, neutral, or unfavorable
    B. will be immediately hostile
    C. will consider his proposals with an open mind
    D. will invariably need an introduction to his subject

11. The one of the following statements that is CORRECT is:
    A. When a stupid question is asked of you by the public, it should be disregarded
    B. If you insist on formality between you and the public, the public will not be able to ask stupid questions that cannot be answered
    C. The public should be treated courteously, regardless of how stupid their questions may be
    D. You should explain to the public how stupid their questions are

12. With regard to public relations, the MOST important item which should be emphasized in an employee training program is that
    A. each inspector is a public relations agent
    B. an inspector should give the public all the information it asks for
    C. it is better to make mistakes and give erroneous information than to tell the public that you do not know the correct answer to their problem
    D. public relations is so specialized a field that only persons specially trained in it should consider it

13. Members of the public frequently ask about departmental procedures.
    Of the following, it is BEST to
    A. advise the public to put the question in writing so that he can get a proper formal reply
    B. refuse to answer because this is a confidential matter
    C. explain the procedure as briefly as possible
    D. attempt to avoid the issue by discussing other matters

14. The effectiveness of a public relations program in a public agency such as the authority is BEST indicated by the
    A. amount of mass media publicity favorable to the policies of the authority
    B. morale of those employees who directly serve the patrons of the authority
    C. public's understanding and support of the authority's program and policies
    D. number of complaint received by the authority from patrons using its facilities

15. In an attempt to improve public opinion about a certain idea, the BEST course of action for an agency to take would be to present the
    A. clearest statements of the idea even though the language is somewhat technical
    B. idea as the result of long-term studies
    C. idea in association with something familiar to most people
    D. idea as the viewpoint of the majority leaders

16. The fundamental factor in any agency's community relations program is
    A. an outline of the objectives
    B. relations with the media
    C. the everyday actions of the employees
    D. a well-planned supervisory program

17. The FUNDAMENTAL factor in the success of a community relations program is
    A. true commitment by the community
    B. true commitment by the administration
    C. a well-planned, systematic approach
    D. the actions of individuals in their contacts with the public

18. The statement below which is LEAST correct is:
    A. Because of selection standards, the supervisor frequently encounters problems resulting from subordinates' inability to express themselves in the language of the profession.
    B. Distortion of the meaning of a communication is usually brought about by a failure to use language that has a precise meaning to others.
    C. The term *filtering* is the distortion or dilution of content of a communication that occurs as information is passed from individual to individual.
    D. The complexity of the *communications net* will directly affect.

19. Consider the following three statements that may or may not be CORRECT:
    I.   In order to prevent the stifling of communications flow, supervisors should insist that employees use the formal communications network.
    II. Two-way communications are faster and more accurate than one-way communications.
    III. There is a direct correlation between the effectiveness of communications and the total setting in which they occur.
    The choice below which MOST accurately describes the above statement is:
    A. All three are correct.
    B. All three are incorrect.
    C. More than one statement is correct.
    D. Only one of the statements is correct.

20. The statement below which is MOST inaccurate is:
    A. The supervisor's most important tool in learning whether or not he is communicating well is feedback.
    B. Follow-up is essential if useful feedback is to be obtained.
    C. Subordinates are entitled, as a matter of right, to explanations from management concerning the reasons for orders or directives.
    D. A skilled supervisor is often able to use the grapevine to good advantage.

21. *Since concurrence by those affected is not sought, this kind of communication can be issued with relative ease.*
    The kind of communication being referred to in this quotation is
    A. autocratic   B. democratic   C. directive   D. free-rein

22. The statement below which is LEAST correct is:
    A. Clarity is more important in oral communicating than in written since the readers of a written communication can read it over again.
    B. Excessive use of abbreviations in written communications should be avoided.
    C. Short sentences with simple words are preferred over complex sentences and difficult words in a written communication.
    D. The *newspaper* style of writing ordinarily simplifies expression and facilitates understanding.

5 (#1)

23. Which one of the following is the MOST important factor for the department to consider in building a good public image?
    A. A good working relationship with the news media
    B. An efficient community relations program
    C. An efficient system for handling citizen complaints
    D. The proper maintenance of facilities and equipment
    E. The behavior of individuals in their contacts with the public.

24. It has been said that the ability to communicate clearly and concisely is the MOST important single skill of the supervisor.
    Consider the following statements:
    I. The adage, *Actions speak louder than words*, has NO application in superior/subordinate communications since good communications are accomplished with words.
    II. The environment in which a communication takes place will *rarely* determine its effect.
    III. Words are symbolic representations which must be associated with past experience or else they are meaningless.
    The choice below which MOST accurately describes the above statements is:
    A. I, II, and III are correct.
    B. I and II are correct, but III is not.
    C. I and III are correct, but II is not.
    D. III is correct, but I and II are not.
    E. I, II, and III are incorrect.

25. According to expert opinion, the effectiveness of an organization is very dependent upon good upward, downward, and lateral communications. Lateral communications are most important to the activity of coordinating the efforts of organizational units. Before real communication can take place at any level, barriers to communication must be recognized, understood, and removed.
    Consider the following three statements:
    I. The *principal* barrier to good communications is a failure to establish empathy between sender and receiver.
    II. The difference in status or rank between the sender and receiver of a communication may be a communications barrier.
    III. Communications are easier if they travel upward from subordinate to superior
    The choice below which MOST accurately describes the above statements is:
    A. I, II and III are incorrect.   B. I and II are incorrect.
    C. I, II, and III are correct.   D. I and II are correct.
    E. I and III are incorrect.

KEY (CORRECT ANSWERS)

1.	B		11.	C
2.	D		12.	A
3.	A		13.	C
4.	A		14.	C
5.	D		15.	C
6.	D		16.	C
7.	A		17.	D
8.	D		18.	A
9.	A		19.	D
10.	A		20.	C

21. A
22. A
23. E
24. D
25. E

EXAMINATION SECTION
TEST 1

DIRECTIONS: Each question or incomplete statement is followed by several suggested answers or completions. Select the one that BEST answers the question or completes the statement. *PRINT THE LETTER OF THE CORRECT ANSWER IN THE SPACE AT THE RIGHT.*

1. In public agencies, communications should be based PRIMARILY on a
   A. two-way flow from the top down and from the bottom up, most of which should be given in writing to avoid ambiguity
   B. multi-direction flow among all levels and with outside persons
   C. rapid, internal one-way flow from the top down
   D. two-way flow of information, most of which should be given orally for purposes of clarity

   1.____

2. In some organizations, changes in policy or procedures are often communicated by word of mouth from supervisors to employees with no prior discussion or exchange of viewpoints with employees.
   This procedure often produces employee dissatisfaction CHIEFLY because
   A. information is mostly unusable since a considerable amount of time is required to transmit information
   B. lower-level supervisors tend to be excessively concerned with minor details
   C. management has failed to seek employees' advice before making changes
   D. valuable staff time is lost between decision-making and the implementation of decisions

   2.____

3. For good letter writing, you should try to visualize the person to whom you are writing, especially if you know him.
   Of the following rules, it is LEAST helpful in such visualization to think of
   A. the person's likes and dislikes, his concerns, and his needs
   B. what you would be likely to say if speaking in person
   C. what you would expect to be asked if speaking in person
   D. your official position in order to be certain that your words are proper

   3.____

4. One approach to good informal letter writing is to make letters and conversational.
   All of the following practices will usually help to do this EXCEPT:
   A. If possible, use a style which is similar to the style used when speaking
   B. Substitute phrases for single words (e.g., *at the present time* for *now*)
   C. Use contractions of words (e.g., *you're* for *you are*)
   D. Use ordinary vocabulary when possible

   4.____

5. All of the following rules will aid in producing clarity in report-writing EXCEPT:
   A. Give specific details or examples, if possible
   B. Keep related words close together in each sentence
   C. Present information in sequential order
   D. Put several thoughts or ideas in each paragraph

6. The one of the following statements about public relations which is MOST accurate is that
   A. in the long run, appearance gains better results than performance
   B. objectivity is decreased if outside public relations consultants are employed
   C. public relations is the responsibility of every employee
   D. public relations should be based on a formal publicity program

7. The form of communication which is usually considered to be MOST personally directed to the intended recipient is the
   A. brochure   B. film   C. letter   D. radio

8. In general, a document that presents an organization's views or opinions on a particular topic is MOST accurately known as a
   A. tear sheet   B. position paper
   C. flyer   D. journal

9. Assume that you have been asked to speak before an organization of persons who oppose a newly announced program in which you are involved. You feel tense about talking to this group.
   Which of the following rules generally would be MOST useful in gaining rapport when speaking before the audience?
   A. Impress them with your experience
   B. Stress all areas of disagreement
   C. Talk to the group as to one person
   D. Use formal grammar and language

10. An organization must have an effective public relations program since, at its best, public relations is a bridge to change.
    All of the following statements about communication and human behavior have validity EXCEPT:
    A. People are more likely to talk about controversial matters with like-minded people than with those holding other views
    B. The earlier an experience, the more powerful its effect since it influences how later experiences will be interpreted
    C. In periods of social tension, official sources gain increased believability
    D. Those who are already interested in a topic are the ones who are most open to receive new communications about it

11. An employee should be encouraged to talk easily and frankly when he is dealing with his supervisor.
    In order to encourage such free communication, it would be MOST appropriate for a supervisor to behave in a(n)
    A. sincere manner; assure the employee that you will deal with him honestly and openly
    B. official manner; you are a supervisor and must always act formally with subordinates
    C. investigative manner; you must probe and question to get to a basis of trust
    D. unemotional manner; the employee's emotions and background should play no part in your dealings with him

11.____

12. Research findings show that an increase in free communication within an agency GENERALLY results in which one of the following?
    A. Improved morale and productivity
    B. Increased promotional opportunities
    C. An increase in authority
    D. A spirit of honesty

12.____

13. Assume that you are a supervisor and your superiors have given you a new-type procedure to be followed.
    Before passing this information on to your subordinates, the one of the following actions that you should take FIRST is to
    A. ask your superiors to send out a memorandum to the entire staff
    B. clarify the procedure in your own mind
    C. set up a training course to provide instruction on the new procedure
    D. write a memorandum to your subordinates

13.____

14. Communication is necessary for an organization to be effective.
    The one of the following which is LEAST important for most communication systems is that
    A. messages are sent quickly and directly to the person who needs them to operate
    B. information should be conveyed understandably and accurately
    C. the method used to transmit information should be kept secret so that security can be maintained
    D. senders of messages must know how their messages are received and acted upon

14.____

15. Which one of the following is the CHIEF advantage of listening willingly to subordinates and encouraging them to talk freely and honestly?
    It
    A. reveals to supervisors the degree to which ideas that are passed down are accepted by subordinates
    B. reduces the participation of subordinates in the operation of the department
    C. encourages subordinates to try for promotion
    D. enables supervisors to learn more readily what the *grapevine* is saying

15.____

16. A supervisor may be informed through either oral or written reports. Which one of the following is an ADVANTAGE of using oral reports?
    A. There is no need for a formal record of the report.
    B. An exact duplicate of the report is not easily transmitted to others.
    C. A good oral report requires little time for preparation.
    D. An oral report involves two-way communication between a subordinate and his supervisor.

17. Of the following, the MOST important reason why supervisors should communicate effectively with the public is to
    A. improve the public's understanding of information that is important for them to know
    B. establish a friendly relationship
    C. obtain information about the kinds of people who come to the agency
    D. convince the public that services are adequate

18. Supervisors should generally NOT use phrases like *too hard*, *too easy*, and *a lot* PRINCIPALLY because such phrases
    A. may be offensive to some minority groups
    B. are too informal
    C. mean different things to different people
    D. are difficult to remember

19. The ability to communicate clearly and concisely is an important element in effective leadership.
    Which of the following statements about oral and written communication is GENERALLY true?
    A. Oral communication is more time-consuming.
    B. Written communication is more likely to be misinterpreted.
    C. Oral communication is useful only in emergencies.
    D. Written communication is useful mainly when giving information to fewer than twenty people.

20. Rumors can often have harmful and disruptive effects on an organization. Which one of the following is the BEST way to prevent rumors from becoming a problem?
    A. Refuse to act on rumors, thereby making them less believable.
    B. Increase the amount of information passed along by the *grapevine*.
    C. Distribute as much factual information as possible.
    D. Provide training in report writing.

21. Suppose that a subordinate asks you about a rumor he has heard. The rumor deals with a subject which your superiors consider *confidential*.
    Which of the following BEST describes how you should answer the subordinate? Tell

A. the subordinate that you don't make the rules and that he should speak to higher ranking officials
B. the subordinate that you will ask your superior for information
C. him only that you cannot comment on the matter
D. him the rumor is not true

22. Supervisors often find it difficult to *get their message across* when instructing newly appointed employees in their various duties.
The MAIN reason for this is generally that the
    A. duties of the employees have increased
    B. supervisor is often so expert in his area that he fails to see it from the learner's point of view
    C. supervisor adapts his instruction to the slowest learner in the group
    D. new employees are younger, less concerned with job security and more interested in fringe benefits

22.____

23. Assume that you are discussing a job problem with an employee under your supervision. During the discussion, you see that the man's eyes are turning away from you and that he is not paying attention.
In order to get the man's attention, you should FIRST
    A. ask him to look you in the eye
    B. talk to him about sports
    C. tell him he is being very rude
    D. change your tone of voice

23.____

24. As a supervisor, you may find it necessary to conduct meetings with your subordinates.
Of the following, which would be MOST helpful in assuring that a meeting accomplishes the purpose for which it was called?
    A. Give notice of the conclusions you would like to reach at the start of the meeting.
    B. Delay the start of the meeting until everyone is present.
    C. Write down points to be discussed in proper sequence.
    D. Make sure everyone is clear on whatever conclusions have been reached and on what must be done after the meeting.

24.____

25. Every supervisor will occasionally be called upon to deliver a reprimand to a subordinate. If done properly, this can greatly help an employee improve his performance.
Which one of the following is NOT a good practice to follow when giving a reprimand?
    A. Maintain your composure and temper
    B. Reprimand a subordinate in the presence of other employees so they can learn the same lesson
    C. Try to understand why the employee was not able to perform satisfactorily
    D. Let your knowledge of the man involved determine the exact nature of the reprimand

25.____

KEY (CORRECT ANSWERS)

1.	C	11.	A
2.	B	12.	A
3.	D	13.	B
4.	B	14.	C
5.	D	15.	A
6.	C	16.	D
7.	C	17.	A
8.	B	18.	C
9.	C	19.	B
10.	C	20.	C

21.	B
22.	B
23.	D
24.	D
25.	B

TEST 2

DIRECTIONS: Each question or incomplete statement is followed by several suggested answers or completions. Select the one that BEST answers the question or completes the statement. *PRINT THE LETTER OF THE CORRECT ANSWER IN THE SPACE AT THE RIGHT.*

1. Usually one thinks of communication as a single step, essentially that of transmitting an idea.
   Actually, however, this is only part of a total process, the FIRST step of which should be
   A. the prompt dissemination of the idea to those who may be affected by it
   B. motivating those affected to take the required action
   C. clarifying the idea in one's own mind
   D. deciding to whom the idea is to be communicated

   1.____

2. Research studies on patterns of informal communication have concluded that most individuals in a group tend to be passive recipients of news, while a few make it their business to spread it around in an organization.
   With this conclusion in mind, it would be MOST correct for the supervisor to attempt to identify these few individuals and
   A. give them the complete facts on important matters in advance of others
   B. inform the other subordinates of the identity of these few individuals so that their influence may be minimized
   C. keep them straight on the facts on important matters
   D. warn them to cease passing along any information to others

   2.____

3. The one of the following which is the PRINCIPAL advantage of making an oral report is that it
   A. affords an immediate opportunity for two-way communication between the subordinate and superior
   B. is an easy method for the superior to use in transmitting information to others of equal rank
   C. saves the time of all concerned
   D. permits more precise pinpointing of praise or blame by means of follow-up questions by the superior

   3.____

4. An agency may sometimes undertake a public relations program of a defensive nature.
   With reference to the use of defensive public relations, it would be MOST correct to state that it
   A. is bound to be ineffective since defensive statements, even though supported by factual data, can never hope to even partly overcome the effects of prior unfavorable attacks
   B. proves that the agency has failed to establish good relationships with newspapers, radio stations, or other means of publicity

   4.____

C. shows that the upper echelons of the agency have failed to develop sound public relations procedures and techniques
D. is sometimes required to aid morale by protecting the agency from unjustified criticism and misunderstanding of policies or procedures

5. Of the following factors which contribute to possible undesirable public attitudes towards an agency, the one which is MOST susceptible to being changed by the efforts of the individual employee in an organization is that
    A. enforcement of unpopular regulations as offended many individuals
    B. the organization itself has an unsatisfactory reputation
    C. the public is not interested in agency matters
    D. there are many errors in judgment committed by individual subordinates

6. It is not enough for an agency's services to be of a high quality; attention must also be given to the acceptability of these services to the general public.
This statement is GENERALLY
    A. *false*; a superior quality of service automatically wins public support
    B. *true*; the agency cannot generally progress beyond the understanding and support of the public
    C. *false*; the acceptance by the public of agency services determines their quality
    D. *true*; the agency is generally unable to engage in any effective enforcement activity without public support

7. Sustained agency participation in a program sponsored by a community organization is MOST justified when
    A. the achievement of agency objectives in some area depends partly on the activity of this organization
    B. the community organization is attempting to widen the base of participation in all community affairs
    C. the agency is uncertain as to what the community wants
    D. the agency is uncertain as to what the community wants

8. Of the following, the LEAST likely way in which a records system may serve a supervisor is in
    A. developing a sympathetic and cooperative public attitude toward the agency
    B. improving the quality of supervision by permitting a check on the accomplishment of subordinates
    C. permit a precise prediction of the exact incidences in specific categories for the following year
    D. helping to take the guesswork out of the distribution of the agency

9. Assuming that the *grapevine* in any organization is virtually indestructible, the one of the following which it is MOST important for management to understand is:
   A. What is being spread by means of the *grapevine* and the reason for spreading it
   B. What is being spread by means of the *grapevine* and how it is being spread
   C. Who is involved in spreading the information that is on the *grapevine*
   D. Why those who are involved in spreading the information are doing so

10. When the supervisor writes a report concerning an investigation to which he has been assigned, it should be LEAST intended to provide
    A. a permanent official record of relevant information gathered
    B. a summary of case findings limited to facts which tend to indicate the guilt of a suspect
    C. a statement of the facts on which higher authorities may base a corrective or disciplinary action
    D. other investigators with information so that they may continue with other phases of the investigation

11. In survey work, questionnaires rather than interviews are sometimes used. The one of the following which is a DISADVANTAGE of the questionnaire method as compared with the interview is the
    A. difficulty of accurately interpreting the results
    B. problem of maintaining anonymity of the participant
    C. fact that it is relatively uneconomical
    D. requirement of special training for the distribution of questionnaires

12. in his contacts with the public, an employee should attempt to create a good climate of support for his agency.
    This statement is GENERALLY
    A. *false*; such attempts are clearly beyond the scope of his responsibility
    B. *true*; employees of an agency who come in contact with the public have the opportunity to affect public relations
    C. *false*; such activity should be restricted to supervisors trained in public relations techniques
    D. *true*; the future expansion of the agency depends to a great extent on continued public support of the agency

13. The repeated use by a supervisor of a call for volunteers to get a job done is objectionable MAINLY because it
    A. may create a feeling of animosity between the volunteers and the non-volunteers
    B. may indicate that the supervisor is avoiding responsibility for making assignments which will be most productive
    C. is an indication that the supervisor is not familiar with the individual capabilities of his men
    D. is unfair to men who, for valid reasons, do not, or cannot volunteer

14. Of the following statements concerning subordinates' expressions to a supervisor of their opinions and feelings concerning work situations, the one which is MOST correct is that
    A. by listening and responding to such expressions the supervisor encourages the development of complaints
    B. the lack of such expressions should indicate to the supervisor that there is a high level of job satisfaction
    C. the more the supervisor listens to and responds to such expressions, the more he demonstrates lack of supervisory ability
    D. by listening and responding to such expressions, the supervisor will enable many subordinates to understand and solve their own problems on the job

14.____

15. In attempting to motivate employees, rewards are considered preferable to punishment PRIMARILY because
    A. punishment seldom has any effect on human behavior
    B. punishment usually results in decreased production
    C. supervisors find it difficult to punish
    D. rewards are more likely to result in willing cooperation

15.____

16. In an attempt to combat the low morale in his organization, a high level supervisor publicized an *open-door policy* to allow employees who wished to do so to come to him with their complaints.
    Which of the following is LEAST likely to account for the fact that no employee came in with a complaint?
    A. Employees are generally reluctant to go over the heads of their immediate supervisor.
    B. The employees did not feel that management would help them.
    C. The low morale was not due to complaints associated with the job.
    D. The employees felt that they had more to lose than to gain.

16.____

17. It is MOST desirable to use written instructions rather than oral instructions for a particular job when
    A. a mistake on the job will not be serious
    B. the job can be completed in a short time
    C. there is no need to explain the job minutely
    D. the job involves many details

17.____

18. If you receive a telephone call regarding a matter which your office does not handle, you should FIRST
    A. give the caller the telephone number of the proper office so that he can dial again
    B. offer to transfer the caller to the proper office
    C. suggest that the caller re-dial since he probably dialed incorrectly
    D. tell the caller he has reached the wrong office and then hang up

18.____

19. When you answer the telephone, the MOST important reason for identifying yourself and your organization is to
    A. give the caller time to collect his or her thoughts
    B. impress the caller with your courtesy
    C. inform the caller that he or she has reached the right number
    D. set a business-like tone at the beginning of the conversation

19._____

20. As soon as you pick up the phone, a very angry caller begins immediately to complain about city agencies and *red tape*. He says that he has been shifted to two or three different offices. It turs out that he is seeking information which is not immediately available to you. You believe, you know, however, where it can be found.
    Which of the following actions is the BEST one for you to take?
    A. To eliminate all confusion, suggest that the caller write the agency stating explicitly what he wants.
    B. Apologize by telling the caller how busy city agencies now are, but also tell him directly that you do not have the information he needs.
    C. Ask for the caller's telephone number and assure him you will call back after you have checked further.
    D. Give the caller the name and telephone number of the person who might be able to help, but explain that you are not positive he will get results/

20._____

21. Which of the following approaches usually provides the BEST communication in the objectives and values of a new program which is to be introduced?
    A. A general written description of the program by the program manager for review by those who share responsibility
    B. An effective verbal presentation by the program manager to those affected
    C. Development of the plan and operational approach in carrying out the program by the program manager assisted by his key subordinates
    D. Development of the plan by the program manager's supervisor

21._____

22. What is the BEST approach for introducing change?
    A
    A. combination of written and also verbal communication to all personnel affected by the change
    B. general bulletin to all personnel
    C. meeting pointing out all the values of the new approach
    D. written directive to key personnel

22._____

23. Of the following, committees are BEST used for
    A. advising the head of the organization
    B. improving functional work
    C. making executive decisions
    D. making specific planning decisions

23._____

24. An effective discussion leader is one who
    A. announces the problem and his preconceived solution at the start of the discussion
    B. guides and directs the discussion according to pre-arranged outline
    C. interrupts or corrects confused participants to save time
    D. permits anyone to say anything at any time

25. The human relations movement in management theory is basically concerned with
    A. counteracting employee unrest
    B. eliminating the *time and motion* man
    C. interrelationships among individuals in organizations
    D. the psychology of the worker

KEY (CORRECT ANSWERS)

1.	C	11.	A
2.	C	12.	B
3.	A	13.	B
4.	D	14.	D
5.	D	15.	D
6.	B	16.	C
7.	A	17.	D
8.	C	18.	B
9.	A	19.	C
10.	B	20.	C

21.	C
22.	A
23.	A
24.	B
25.	C

READING COMPREHENSION
UNDERSTANDING AND INTERPRETING WRITTEN MATERIAL
EXAMINATION SECTION
TEST 1

DIRECTIONS: Each question or incomplete statement is followed by several suggested answers or completions. Select the one that BEST answers the question or completes the statement. *PRINT THE LETTER OF THE CORRECT ANSWER IN THE SPACE AT THE RIGHT.*

Questions 1-3.

DIRECTIONS: Questions 1 through 3 are to be answered SOLELY on the basis of the following statement.

The equipment in a mailroom may include a mail metering machine. This machine simultaneously stamps, postmarks, seals, and counts letters as fast as the operator can feed them. It can also print the proper postage directly on a gummed strip to be affixed to bulky items. It is equipped with a meter which is removed from the machine and sent to the postmaster to be set for a given number of stampings of any denomination. The setting of the meter must be paid for in advance. One of the advantages of metered mail is that it bypasses the cancellation operation and thereby facilitates handling by the post office. Mail metering also makes the pilfering of stamps impossible, but does not prevent the passage of personal mail in company envelopes through the meters unless there is established a rigid control or censorship over outgoing mail.

1. According to this statement, the postmaster

    A. is responsible for training new clerks in the use of mail metering machines
    B. usually recommends that both large and small firms adopt the use of mail metering machines
    C. is responsible for setting the meter to print a fixed number of stampings
    D. examines the mail metering machine to see that they are properly installed in the mailroom

2. According to this statement, the use of mail metering machines

    A. requires the employment of more clerks in a mailroom than does the use of postage stamps
    B. interferes with the handling of large quantities of outgoing mail
    C. does not prevent employees from sending their personal letters at company expense
    D. usually involves smaller expenditures for mailroom equipment than does the use of postage stamps

3. On the basis of this statement, it is MOST accurate to state that

    A. mail metering machines are often used for opening envelopes
    B. postage stamps are generally used when bulky packages are to be mailed
    C. the use of metered mail tends to interfere with rapid mail handling by the post office
    D. mail metering machines can seal and count letters at the same time

Questions 4-5.

DIRECTIONS: Questions 4 and 5 are to be answered SOLELY on the basis of the following statement.

Forms are printed sheets of paper on which information is to be entered. While what is printed on the form is most important, the kind of paper used in making the form is also important. The kind of paper should be selected with regard to the use to which the form will be subjected. Printing a form on an unnecessarily expensive grade of papers is wasteful. On the other hand, using too cheap or flimsy a form can materially interfere with satisfactory performance of the work the form is being planned to do. Thus, a form printed on both sides normally requires a heavier paper than a form printed only on one side. Forms to be used as permanent records, or which are expected to have a very long life in files, requires a quality of paper which will not disintegrate or discolor with age. A form which will go through a great deal of handling requires a strong, tough paper, while thinness is a necessary qualification where the making of several copies of a form will be required.

4. According to this statement, the type of paper used for making forms

    A. should be chosen in accordance with the use to which the form will be put
    B. should be chosen before the type of printing to be used has been decided upon
    C. is as important as the information which is printed on it
    D. should be strong enough to be used for any purpose

5. According to this statement, forms that are

    A. printed on both sides are usually economical and desirable
    B. to be filed permanently should not deteriorate as time goes on
    C. expected to last for a long time should be handled carefully
    D. to be filed should not be printed on inexpensive paper

Questions 6-8.

DIRECTIONS: Questions 6 through 8 are to be answered SOLELY on the basis of the following paragraph.

The increase in the number of public documents in the last two centuries closely matches the increase in population in the United States. The great number of public documents has become a serious threat to their usefulness. It is necessary to have programs which will reduce the number of public documents that are kept and which will, at the same time, assure keeping those that have value. Such programs need a great deal of thought to have any success.

6. According to the above paragraph, public documents may be LESS useful if

    A. the files are open to the public
    B. the record room is too small
    C. the copying machine is operated only during normal working hours
    D. too many records are being kept

7. According to the above paragraph, the growth of the population in the United States has matched the growth in the quantity of public documents for a period of MOST NEARLY _____ years.

   A. 50   B. 100   C. 200   D. 300

8. According to the above paragraph, the increased number of public documents has made it necessary to

   A. find out which public documents are worth keeping
   B. reduce the great number of public documents by decreasing government services
   C. eliminate the copying of all original public documents
   D. avoid all new copying devices

Questions 9-10.

DIRECTIONS: Questions 9 and 10 are to be answered SOLELY on the basis of the following paragraph.

The work goals of an agency can best be reached if the employees understand and agree with these goals. One way to gain such understanding and agreement is for management to encourage and seriously consider suggestions from employees in the setting of agency goals.

9. On the basis of the above paragraph, the BEST way to achieve the work goals of an agency is to

   A. make certain that employees work as hard as possible
   B. study the organizational structure of the agency
   C. encourage employees to think seriously about the agency's problems
   D. stimulate employee understanding of the work goals

10. On the basis of the above paragraph, understanding and agreement with agency goals can be gained by

    A. allowing the employees to set agency goals
    B. reaching agency goals quickly
    C. legislative review of agency operations
    D. employee participation in setting agency goals

Questions 11-13.

DIRECTIONS: Questions 11 through 13 are to be answered SOLELY on the basis of the following paragraph.

In order to organize records properly, it is necessary to start from their very beginning and trace each copy of the record to find out how it is used, how long it is used, and what may finally be done with it. Although several copies of the record are made, one copy should be marked as the copy of record. This is the formal legal copy, held to meet the requirements of the law. The other copies may be retained for brief periods for reference purposes, but these copies should not be kept after their usefulness as reference ends. There is another reason for tracing records through the office and that is to determine how long it takes the copy of record to reach the central file. The copy of record must not be kept longer than necessary by the section of the office which has prepared it, but should be sent to the central file as soon as possible so that it can be available to the various sections of the office. The central file can make the copy of record available to the various sections of the office at an early date only if it arrives at the central file as quickly as possible. Just as soon as its immediate or active service period is ended, the copy of record should be removed from the central file and put into the inactive file in the office to be stored for whatever length of time may be necessary to meet legal requirements, and then destroyed.

11. According to the above paragraph, a reason for tracing records through an office is to

    A. determine how long the central file must keep the records
    B. organize records properly
    C. find out how many copies of each record are required
    D. identify the copy of record

12. According to the above paragraph, in order for the central file to have the copy of record available as soon as possible for the various sections of the office, it is MOST important that the

    A. copy of record to be sent to the central file meets the requirements of the law
    B. copy of record is not kept in the inactive file too long
    C. section preparing the copy of record does not unduly delay in sending it to the central file
    D. central file does not keep the copy of record beyond its active service period

13. According to the above paragraph, the length of time a copy of a record is kept in the inactive file of an office depends CHIEFLY on the

    A. requirements of the law
    B. length of time that is required to trace the copy of record through the office
    C. use that is made of the copy of record
    D. length of the period that the copy of record is used for reference purposes

Questions 14-16.

DIRECTIONS: Questions 14 through 16 are to be answered SOLELY on the basis of the following paragraph.

The office was once considered as nothing more than a focal point of internal and external correspondence. It was capable only of dispatching a few letters upon occasion and of preparing records of little practical value. Under such a concept, the vitality of the office force was impaired. Initiative became stagnant, and the lot of the office worker was not likely to be a happy one. However, under the new concept of office management, the possibilities of waste and mismanagement in office operation are now fully recognized, as are the possibilities for the modern office to assist in the direction and control of business operations. Fortunately, the modern concept of the office as a centralized service-rendering unit is gaining ever greater acceptance in today's complex business world, for without the modern office, the production wheels do not turn and the distribution of goods and services is not possible.

14. According to the above paragraph, the fundamental difference between the old and the new concept of the office is the change in the

    A. accepted functions of the office
    B. content and the value of the records kept
    C. office methods and systems
    D. vitality and morale of the office force

15. According to the above paragraph, an office operated today under the old concept of the office MOST likely would

    A. make older workers happy in their jobs
    B. be part of an old thriving business concern
    C. have a passive role in the conduct of a business enterprise
    D. attract workers who do not believe in modern methods

16. Of the following, the MOST important implication of the above paragraph is that a present-day business organization cannot function effectively without the

    A. use of modern office equipment
    B. participation and cooperation of the office
    C. continued modernization of office procedures
    D. employment of office workers with skill and initiative

Questions 17-20.

DIRECTIONS: Questions 17 through 20 are to be answered SOLELY on the basis of the following paragraph.

A report is frequently ineffective because the person writing it is not fully acquainted with all the necessary details before he actually starts to construct the report. All details pertaining to the subject should be known before the report is started. If the essential facts are not known, they should be investigated. It is wise to have essential facts written down rather than to depend too much on memory, especially if the facts pertain to such matters as amounts, dates, names of persons, or other specific data. When the necessary information has been gathered, the general plan and content of the report should be thought out before the writing is actually begun. A person with little or no experience in writing reports may find that it is wise to make a brief outline. Persons with more experience should not need a written outline, but they should make mental notes of the steps they are to follow. If writing reports without dictation is a regular part of an office worker's duties, he should set aside a certain time during the day when he is least likely to be interrupted. That may be difficult, but in most offices there are certain times in the day when the callers, telephone calls, and other interruptions are not numerous. During those times, it is best to write reports that need undivided concentration. Reports that are written amid a series of interruptions may be poorly done.

17. Before starting to write an effective report, it is necessary to

    A. memorize all specific information
    B. disregard ambiguous data
    C. know all pertinent information
    D. develop a general plan

18. Reports dealing with complex and difficult material should be

   A. prepared and written by the supervisor of the unit
   B. written when there is the least chance of interruption
   C. prepared and written as part of regular office routine
   D. outlined and then dictated

19. According to the paragraph, employees with no prior familiarity in writing reports may find it helpful to

   A. prepare a brief outline
   B. mentally prepare a synopsis of the report's content
   C. have a fellow employee help in writing the report
   D. consult previous reports

20. In writing a report, needed information which is unclear should be

   A. disregarded
   B. memorized
   C. investigated
   D. gathered

Questions 21-25.

DIRECTIONS: Questions 21 through 25 are to be answered SOLELY on the basis of the following passage.

Positive discipline minimizes the amount of personal supervision required and aids in the maintenance of standards. When a new employee has been properly introduced and carefully instructed, when he has come to know the supervisor and has confidence in the supervisor's ability to take care of him, when he willingly cooperates with the supervisor, that employee has been under positive discipline and can be put on his own to produce the quantity and quality of work desired. Negative discipline, the fear of transfer to a less desirable location, for example, to a limited extent may restrain certain individuals from overt violation of rules and regulations governing attendance and conduct which in governmental agencies are usually on at least an agency-wide basis. Negative discipline may prompt employees to perform according to certain rules to avoid a penalty such as, for example, docking for tardiness.

21. According to the above passage, it is reasonable to assume that in the area of discipline, the first-line supervisor in a governmental agency has GREATER scope for action in

   A. *positive* discipline, because negative discipline is largely taken care of by agency rules and regulations
   B. *negative* discipline, because rules and procedures are already fixed and the supervisor can rely on them
   C. *positive* discipline, because the supervisor is in a position to recommend transfers
   D. *negative* discipline, because positive discipline is reserved for people on a higher supervisory level

22. In order to maintain positive discipline of employees under his supervision, it is MOST important for a supervisor to

   A. assure each employee that he has nothing to worry about
   B. insist at the outset on complete cooperation from employees

C. be sure that each employee is well trained in his job
D. inform new employees of the penalties for not meeting standards

23. According to the above passage, a feature of negative discipline is that it

    A. may lower employee morale
    B. may restrain employees from disobeying the rules
    C. censures equal treatment of employees
    D. tends to create standards for quality of work

24. A REASONABLE conclusion based on the above passage is that positive discipline benefits a supervisor because

    A. he can turn over orientation and supervision of a new employee to one of his subordinates
    B. subordinates learn to cooperate with one another when working on an assignment
    C. it is easier to administer
    D. it cuts down, in the long run, on the amount of time the supervisor needs to spend on direct supervision

25. Based on the above passage, it is REASONABLE to assume, that an important difference between positive discipline and negative discipline is that positive discipline

    A. is concerned with the quality of work and negative discipline with the quantity of work
    B. leads to a more desirable basis for motivation of the employee
    C. is more likely to be concerned with agency rules and regulations
    D. uses fear while negative discipline uses penalties to prod employees to adequate performance

KEY (CORRECT ANSWERS)

1.	C	11.	B
2.	C	12.	C
3.	D	13.	A
4.	A	14.	A
5.	B	15.	C
6.	D	16.	B
7.	C	17.	C
8.	A	18.	B
9.	D	19.	A
10.	D	20.	B

21. A
22. C
23. B
24. D
25. B

TEST 2

Questions 1-6.

DIRECTIONS: Questions 1 through 6 are to be answered SOLELY on the basis of the following passage.

Inherent in all organized endeavors is the need to resolve the individual differences involved in conflict. Conflict may be either a positive or negative factor since it may lead to creativity, innovation and progress on the one hand, or it may result, on the other hand, in a deterioration or even destruction of the organization. Thus, some forms of conflict are desirable, whereas others are undesirable and ethically wrong.

There are three management strategies which deal with interpersonal conflict. In the *divide-and-rule strategy,* management attempts to maintain control by limiting the conflict to those directly involved and preventing their disagreement from spreading to the larger group. The *suppression-of-differences strategy* entails ignoring conflicts or pretending they are irrelevant. In the *working-through-differences strategy,* management actively attempts to solve or resolve intergroup or interpersonal conflicts. Of the three strategies, only the last directly attacks and has the potential for eliminating the causes of conflict. An essential part of this strategy, however, is its employment by a committed and relatively mature management team.

1. According to the above passage, the *divide-and-rule strategy for* dealing with conflict is the attempt to

   A. involve other people in the conflict
   B. restrict the conflict to those participating in it
   C. divide the conflict into positive and negative factors
   D. divide the conflict into a number of smaller ones

2. The word *conflict* is used in relation to both positive and negative factors in this passage. Which one of the following words is MOST likely to describe the activity which the word *conflict,* in the sense of the passage, implies?

   A. Competition   B. Confusion
   C. Cooperation   D. Aggression

3. According to the above passage, which one of the following characteristics is shared by both the *suppression-of-differences strategy* and the *divide-and-rule strategy*?

   A. Pretending that conflicts are irrelevant
   B. Preventing conflicts from spreading to the group situation
   C. Failure to directly attack the causes of conflict
   D. Actively attempting to resolve interpersonal conflict

4. According to the above passage, the successful resolution of interpersonal conflict requires

   A. allowing the group to mediate conflicts between two individuals
   B. division of the conflict into positive and negative factors
   C. involvement of a committed, mature management team
   D. ignoring minor conflicts until they threaten the organization

5. Which can be MOST reasonably inferred from the above passage? Conflict between two individuals is LEAST likely to continue when management uses

   A. the *working-through differences strategy*
   B. the *suppression-of differences strategy*
   C. the *divide-and-rule strategy*
   D. a combination of all three strategies

6. According to the above passage, a DESIRABLE result of conflict in an organization is when conflict

   A. exposes production problems in the organization
   B. can be easily ignored by management
   C. results in advancement of more efficient managers
   D. leads to development of new methods

Questions 7-13.

DIRECTIONS: Questions 7 through 13 are to be answered SOLELY on the basis of the passage below.

Modern management places great emphasis on the concept of communication. The communication process consists of the steps through which an idea or concept passes from its inception by one person, the sender, until it is acted upon by another person, the receiver. Through an understanding of these steps and some of the possible barriers that may occur, more effective communication may be achieved. The first step in the communication process is ideation by the sender. This is the formation of the intended content of the message he wants to transmit. In the next step, encoding, the sender organizes his ideas into a series of symbols designed to communicate his message to his intended receiver. He selects suitable words or phrases that can be understood by the receiver, and he also selects the appropriate media to be used—for example, memorandum, conference, etc. The third step is transmission of the encoded message through selected channels in the organizational structure. In the fourth step, the receiver enters the process by tuning in to receive the message. If the receiver does not function, however, the message is lost. For example, if the message is oral, the receiver must be a good listener. The fifth step is decoding of the message by the receiver, as for example, by changing words into ideas. At this step, the decoded message may not be the same idea that the sender originally encoded because the sender and receiver have different perceptions regarding the meaning of certain words. Finally, the receiver acts or responds. He may file the information, ask for more information, or take other action. There can be no assurance, however, that communication has taken place unless there is some type of feedback to the sender in the form of an acknowledgement that the message was received.

7. According to the above passage, *ideation* is the process by which the

   A. sender develops the intended content of the message
   B. sender organizes his ideas into a series of symbols
   C. receiver tunes in to receive the message
   D. receiver decodes the message

8. In the last sentence of the passage, the word *feedback* refers to the process by which the sender is assured that the

   A. receiver filed the information
   B. receiver's perception is the same as his own
   C. message was received
   D. message was properly interpreted

9. Which one of the following BEST shows the order of the steps in the communication process as described in the passage?

   A. 1 - ideation   2 - encoding
      3 - decoding   4 - transmission
      5 - receiving   6 - action
      7 - feedback to the sender

   B. 1 - ideation   2 - encoding
      3 - transmission 4 - decoding
      5 - receiving   6 - action
      7 - feedback to the sender

   C. 1 - ideation   2 - decoding
      3 - transmission 4 - receiving
      5 - encoding   6 - action
      7 - feedback to the sender

   D. 1 - ideation   2 - encoding
      3 - transmission 4 - receiving
      5 - decoding   6 - action
      7 - feedback to the sender

10. Which one of the following BEST expresses the main theme of the passage?

    A. Different individuals have the same perceptions regarding the meaning of words.
    B. An understanding of the steps in the communication process may achieve better communication.
    C. Receivers play a passive role in the communication process.
    D. Senders should not communicate with receivers who transmit feedback.

11. The above passage implies that a receiver does NOT function properly when he

    A. transmits feedback   B. files the information
    C. is a poor listener   D. asks for more information

12. Which one of the following, according to the above passage, is included in the SECOND step of the communication process?

    A. Selecting the appropriate media to be used in transmission
    B. Formulation of the intended content of the message
    C. Using appropriate media to respond to the receiver's feedback
    D. Transmitting the message through selected channels in the organization

13. The above passage implies that the *decoding process* is MOST NEARLY the reverse of the _____ process.

    A. transmission   B. receiving
    C. feedback   D. encoding

Questions 14-19.

DIRECTIONS: Questions 14 through 19 are to be answered SOLELY on the basis of the following passage.

It is often said that no system will work if the people who carry it out do not want it to work. In too many cases, a departmental reorganization that seemed technically sound and economically practical has proved to be a failure because the planners neglected to take the human factor into account. The truth is that employees are likely to feel threatened when they learn that a major change is in the wind. It does not matter whether or not the change actually poses a threat to an employee; the fact that he believes it does or fears it might is enough to make him feel insecure. Among the dangers he fears, the foremost is the possibility that his job may cease to exist and that he may be laid off or shunted into a less skilled position at lower pay. Even if he knows that his own job category is secure, however, he is likely to fear losing some of the important intangible advantages of his present position—for instance, he may fear that he will be separated from his present companions and thrust in with a group of strangers, or that he will find himself in a lower position on the organizational ladder if a new position is created above his.

It is important that management recognize these natural fears and take them into account in planning any kind of major change. While there is no cut-and-dried formula for preventing employee resistance, there are several steps that can be taken to reduce employees' fears and gain their cooperation. First, unwarranted fears can be dispelled if employees are kept informed of the planning from the start and if they know exactly what to expect. Next, assurance on matters such as retraining, transfers, and placement help should be given as soon as it is clear what direction the reorganization will take. Finally, employees' participation in the planning should be actively sought. There is a great psychological difference between feeling that a change is being forced upon one from the outside, and feeling that one is an insider who is helping to bring about a change.

14. According to the above passage, employees who are not in real danger of losing their jobs because of a proposed reorganization

    A. will be eager to assist in the reorganization
    B. will pay little attention to the reorganization
    C. should not be taken into account in planning the reorganization
    D. are nonetheless likely to feel threatened by the reorganization

15. The passage mentions the *intangible advantages* of a position.
    Which of the following BEST describes the kind of advantages alluded to in the passage?

    A. Benefits such as paid holidays and vacations
    B. Satisfaction of human needs for things like friendship and status
    C. Qualities such as leadership and responsibility
    D. A work environment that meets satisfactory standards of health and safety

16. According to the passage, an employee's fear that a reorganization may separate him from his present companions is a (n)

    A. childish and immature reaction to change
    B. unrealistic feeling since this is not going to happen

C. possible reaction that the planners should be aware of
D. incentive to employees to participate in the planning

17. On the basis of the above passage, it would be DESIRABLE, when planning a departmental reorganization, to

    A. be governed by employee feelings and attitudes
    B. give some employees lower positions
    C. keep employees informed
    D. lay off those who are less skilled

17._____

18. What does the passage say can be done to help gain employees' cooperation in a reorganization?

    A. Making sure that the change is technically sound, that it is economically practical, and that the human factor is taken into account
    B. Keeping employees fully informed, offering help in fitting them into new positions, and seeking their participation in the planning
    C. Assuring employees that they will not be laid off, that they will not be reassigned to a group of strangers, and that no new positions will be created on the organization ladder
    D. Reducing employees' fears, arranging a retraining program, and providing for transfers

18._____

19. Which of the following suggested titles would be MOST appropriate for this passage?

    A. PLANNING A DEPARTMENTAL REORGANIZATION
    B. WHY EMPLOYEES ARE AFRAID
    C. LOOKING AHEAD TO THE FUTURE
    D. PLANNING FOR CHANGE: THE HUMAN FACTOR

19._____

Questions 20-22.

DIRECTIONS: Questions 20 through 22 are to be answered SOLELY on the basis of the following passage.

The achievement of good human relations is essential if a business office is to produce at top efficiency and is to be a pleasant place in which to work. All office workers plan an important role in handling problems in human relations. They should, therefore, strive to acquire the understanding, tactfulness, and awareness necessary to deal effectively with actual office situations involving co-workers on all levels. Only in this way can they truly become responsible, interested, cooperative, and helpful members of the staff.

20. The selection implies that the MOST important value of good human relations in an office is to develop

    A. efficiency   B. cooperativeness
    C. tact   D. pleasantness and efficiency

20._____

21. Office workers should acquire understanding in dealing with

    A. co-workers   B. subordinates
    C. superiors   D. all members of the staff

21._____

22. The selection indicates that a highly competent secretary who is also very argumentative is meeting office requirements   22.____

    A. wholly
    B. partly
    C. slightly
    D. not at all

Questions 23-25.

DIRECTIONS: Questions 23 through 25 are to be answered SOLELY on the basis of the following passage.

It is common knowledge that ability to do a particular job and performance on the job do not always go hand in hand. Persons with great potential abilities sometimes fall down on the job because of laziness or lack of interest in the job, while persons with mediocre talents have often achieved excellent results through their industry and their loyalty to the interests of their employers. It is clear; therefore, that in a balanced personnel program, measures of employee ability need to be supplemented by measures of employee performance, for the final test of any employee is his performance on the job.

23. The MOST accurate of the following statements, on the basis of the above paragraph, is that   23.____

    A. employees who lack ability are usually not industrious
    B. an employee's attitudes are more important than his abilities
    C. mediocre employees who are interested in their work are preferable to employees who possess great ability
    D. superior capacity for performance should be supplemented with proper attitudes

24. On the basis of the above paragraph, the employee of most value to his employer is NOT necessarily the one who   24.____

    A. best understands the significance of his duties
    B. achieves excellent results
    C. possesses the greatest talents
    D. produces the greatest amount of work

25. According to the above paragraph, an employee's efficiency is BEST determined by an   25.____

    A. appraisal of his interest in his work
    B. evaluation of the work performed by him
    C. appraisal of his loyalty to his employer
    D. evaluation of his potential ability to perform his work

KEY (CORRECT ANSWERS)

1. B
2. A
3. C
4. C
5. A

6. D
7. A
8. C
9. D
10. B

11. C
12. A
13. D
14. D
15. B

16. C
17. C
18. B
19. D
20. D

21. D
22. B
23. D
24. C
25. B

TEST 3

Questions 1-8.

DIRECTIONS: Questions 1 through 8 are to be answered SOLELY on the basis of the following information and directions.

Assume that you are a clerk in a city agency. Your supervisor has asked you to classify each of the accidents that happened to employees in the agency into the following five categories:

A. An accident that occurred in the period from January through June, between 9 A.M. and 12 Noon, that was the result of carelessness on the part of the injured employee, that caused the employee to lose less than seven working hours, that happened to an employee who was 40 years of age or over, and who was employed in the agency for less than three years;

B. An accident that occurred in the period from July through December, after 1 P.M., that was the result of unsafe conditions, that caused the injured employee to lose less than seven working hours, that happened to an employee who was 40 years of age or over, and who was employed in the agency for three years or more;

C. An accident that occurred in the period from January through June, after 1 P.M., that was the result of carelessness on the part of the injured employee, that caused the injured employee to lose seven or more working hours, that happened to an employee who was less than 40 years old, and who was employed in the agency for three years or more;

D. An accident that occurred in the period from July through December, between 9 A.M. and 12 Noon, that was the result of unsafe conditions, that caused the injured employee to lose seven or more working hours, that happened to an employee who was less than 40 years old, and who was employed in the agency for less than three years;

E. Accidents that cannot be classified in any of the foregoing groups. NOTE: In classifying these accidents, an employee's age and length of service are computed as of the date of accident. In all cases, it is to be assumed that each employee has been employed continuously in city service, and that each employee works seven hours a day, from 9 A.M. to 5 P.M., with lunch from 12 Noon to 1 P.M. In each question, consider only the information which will assist you in classifying the accident. Any information which is of no assistance in classifying an accident should not be considered.

1. The unsafe condition of the stairs in the building caused Miss Perkins to have an accident on October 14, 2003 at 4 P.M. When she returned to work the following day at 1 P.M., Miss Perkins said that the accident was the first one that had occurred to her in her ten years of employment with the agency. She was born on April 27, 1962.

1.____

2. On the day after she completed her six-month probationary period of employment with the agency, Miss Green, who had been considered a careful worker by her supervisor, injured her left foot in an accident caused by her own carelessness. She went home immediately after the accident, which occurred at 10 A.M., March 19, 2004, but returned to work at the regular time on the following morning. Miss Green was born July 12, 1963 in New York City.

2.____

3. The unsafe condition of a duplicating machine caused Mr. Martin to injure himself in an accident on September 8, 2006 at 2 P.M. As a result of the accident, he was unable to work the remainder of the day, but returned to his office ready for work on the following morning. Mr. Martin, who has been working for the agency since April 1, 2003, was born in St. Louis on February 1, 1968.   3.____

4. Mr. Smith was hospitalized for two weeks because of a back injury resulted from an accident on the morning of November 16, 2006. Investigation of the accident revealed that it was caused by the unsafe condition of the floor on which Mr. Smith had been walking. Mr. Smith, who is an accountant, has been anemployee of the agency since March 1, 2004, and was born in Ohio on June 10, 1968.   4.____

5. Mr. Allen cut his right hand because he was careless in operating a multilith machine. Mr. Allen, who was 33 years old when the accident took place, has been employed by the agency since August 17, 1992. The accident, which occurred on January 26, 2006, at 2 P.M., caused Mr. Allen to be absent from work for the rest of the day. He was able to return to work the next morning.   5.____

6. Mr. Rand, who is a college graduate, was born on December, 28, 1967, and has been working for the agency since January 7, 2002. On Monday, April 25, 2005, at 2 P.M., his carelessness in operating a duplicating machine caused him to have an accident and to be sent home from work immediately. Fortunately, he was able to return to work at his regular time on the following Wednesday.   6.____

7. Because he was careless in running down a flight of stairs, Mr. Brown fell, bruising his right hand. Although the accident occurred shortly after he arrived for work on the morning of May 22, 2006, he was unable to resume work until 3 P.M. that day. Mr. Brown was born on August 15, 1955, and began working for the agency on September 12, 2003, as a clerk, at a salary of $22,750 per annum.   7.____

8. On December 5, 2005, four weeks after he had begun working for the agency, the unsafe condition of an automatic stapling machine caused Mr. Thomas to injure himself in an accident. Mr. Thomas, who was born on May 19,1975, lost three working days because of the accident, which occurred at 11:45 A.M.   8.____

Questions 9-10.

DIRECTIONS: Questions 9 and 10 are to be answered SOLELY on the basis of the following paragraph.

An impending reorganization within an agency will mean loss by transfer of several professional staff members from the personnel division. The division chief is asked to designate the persons to be transferred. After reviewing the implications of this reduction of staff with his assistant, the division chief discusses the matter at a staff meeting. He adopts the recommendations of several staff members to have volunteers make up the required reduction.

9. The decision to permit personnel to volunteer for transfer is

   A. *poor;* it is not likely that the members of a division are of equal value to the division chief
   B. *good;* dissatisfied members will probably be more productive elsewhere
   C. *poor;* the division chief has abdicated his responsibility to carry out the order given to him
   D. *good;* morale among remaining staff is likely to improve in a more cohesive framework

10. Suppose that one of the volunteers is a recently appointed employee who has completed his probationary period acceptably, but whose attitude toward division operations and agency administration tends to be rather negative and sometimes even abrasive. Because of his lack of commitment to the division, his transfer is recommended. If the transfer is approved, the division chief should, prior to the transfer,

    A. discuss with the staff the importance of commitment to the work of the agency and its relationship with job satisfaction
    B. refrain from any discussion of attitude with the employee
    C. discuss with the employee his concern about the employee's attitude
    D. avoid mention of attitude in the evaluation appraisal prepared for the receiving division chief

Questions 11-16.

DIRECTIONS: Questions 11 through 16 are to be answered SOLELY on the basis of the following paragraph.

   Methods of administration of office activities, much of which consists of providing information and *know-how* needed to coordinate both activities within that particular office and other offices, have been among the last to come under the spotlight of management analysis. Progress has been rapid during the past decade, however, and is now accelerating at such a pace that an *information revolution* in office management appears to be in the making. Although triggered by technological breakthroughs in electronic computers and other giant steps in mechanization, this information revolution must be attributed to underlying forces, such as the increased complexity of both governmental and private enterprise, and ever-keener competition. Size, diversification, specialization of function, and decentralization are among the forces which make coordination of activities both more imperative and more difficult. Increased competition, both domestic and international, leaves little margin for error in managerial decisions. Several developments during recent years indicate an evolving pattern. In 1960, the American Management Association expanded the scope of its activities and changed the name of its Office Management Division to Administrative Services Division. Also in 1960, the magazine *Office Management* merged with the magazine *American Business,* and this new publication was named *Administrative Management.*

11. A REASONABLE inference that can be made from the information in the above paragraph is that an important role of the office manager today is to

    A. work toward specialization of functions performed by his subordinates
    B. inform and train subordinates regarding any new developments in computer technology and mechanization
    C. assist the professional management analysts with the management analysis work in the organization
    D. supply information that can be used to help coordinate and manage the other activities of the organization

11._____

12. An IMPORTANT reason for the *information revolution* that has been taking place in office management is the

    A. advance made in management analysis in the past decade
    B. technological breakthrough in electronic computers and mechanization
    C. more competitive and complicated nature of private business and government
    D. increased efficiency of office management techniques in the past ten years

12._____

13. According to the above paragraph, specialization of function in an organization is MOST likely to result in

    A. the elimination of errors in managerial decisions
    B. greater need to coordinate activities
    C. more competition with other organizations, both domestic and international
    D. a need for office managers with greater flexibility

13._____

14. The word *evolving,* as used in the third from last sentence in the above paragraph, means MOST NEARLY

    A. developing by gradual changes
    B. passing on to others
    C. occurring periodically
    D. breaking up into separate, constituent parts

14._____

15. Of the following, the MOST reasonable implication of the changes in names mentioned in the last part of the above paragraph is that these groups are attempting to

    A. professionalize the field of office management and the title of Office Manager
    B. combine two publications into one because of the increased costs of labor and materials
    C. adjust to the fact that the field of office management is broadening
    D. appeal to the top managerial people rather than the office management people in business and government

15._____

16. According to the above paragraph, intense competition among domestic and international enterprises makes it MOST important for an organization's managerial staff to

    A. coordinate and administer office activities with other activities in the organization
    B. make as few errors in decision-making as possible
    C. concentrate on decentralization and reduction of size of the individual divisions of the organization
    D. restrict decision-making only to top management officials

16._____

Questions 17-21.

DIRECTIONS: Questions 17 through 21 are to be answered SOLELY on the basis of the following passage.

For some office workers, it is useful to be familiar with the four main classes of domestic mail; for others, it is essential. Each class has a different rate of postage, and some have requirements concerning wrapping, sealing, or special information to be placed on the package. First class mail, the class which may not be opened for postal inspection, includes letters, postcards, business reply cards, and other kinds of written matter. There are different rates for some of the kinds of cards which can be sent by first class mail. The maximum weight for an item sent by first class mail is 70 pounds. An item which is not letter size should be marked *First Class* on all sides. Although office workers most often come into contact with first class mail, they may find it helpful to know something about the other classes. Second class mail is generally used for mailing newspapers and magazines. Publishers of these articles must meet certain U.S. Postal Service requirements in order to obtain a permit to use second class mailing rates. Third class mail, which must weigh less than 1 pound, includes printed materials and merchandise parcels. There are two rate structures for this class - a single piece rate and a bulk rate. Fourth class mail, also known as parcel post, includes packages weighing from one to 40 pounds. For more information about these classes of mail and the actual mailing rates, contact your local post office.

17. According to this passage, first class mail is the *only* class which   17.____

    A. has a limit on the maximum weight of an item
    B. has different rates for items within the class
    C. may not be opened for postal inspection
    D. should be used by office workers

18. According to this passage, the one of the following items which may CORRECTLY be sent by fourth class mail is a   18.____

    A. magazine weighing one-half pound
    B. package weighing one-half pound
    C. package weighing two pounds
    D. postcard

19. According to this passage, there are different postage rates for   19.____

    A. a newspaper sent by second class mail and a magazine sent by second class mail
    B. each of the classes of mail
    C. each pound of fourth class mail
    D. printed material sent by third class mail and merchandise parcels sent by third class mail

20. In order to send a newspaper by second class mail, a publisher MUST   20.____

    A. have met certain postal requirements and obtained a permit
    B. indicate whether he wants to use the single piece or the bulk rate
    C. make certain that the newspaper weighs less than one pound
    D. mark the newspaper *Second Class* on the top and bottom of the wrapper

21. Of the following types of information, the one which is NOT mentioned in the passage is the

    A. class of mail to which parcel post belongs
    B. kinds of items which can be sent by each class of mail
    C. maximum weight for an item sent by fourth class mail
    D. postage rate for each of the four classes of mail

Questions 22-25.

DIRECTIONS: Questions 22 through 25 are to be answered SOLELY on the basis of the following paragraph.

A standard comprises characteristics attached to an aspect of a process or product by which it can be evaluated. Standardization is the development and adoption of standards. When they are formulated, standards are not usually the product of a single person, but represent the thoughts and ideas of a group, leavened with the knowledge and information which are currently available. Standards which do not meet certain basic requirements become a hindrance rather than an aid to progress. Standards must not only be correct, accurate, and precise in requiring no more and no less than what is needed for satisfactory results, but they must also be workable in the sense that their usefulness is not nullified by external conditions. Standards should also be acceptable to the people who use them. If they are not acceptable, they cannot be considered to be satisfactory, although they may possess all the other essential characteristics.

22. According to the above paragraph, a processing standard that requires the use of materials that cannot be procured is MOST likely to be

    A. incomplete   B. unworkable
    C. inaccurate   D. unacceptable

23. According to the above paragraph, the construction of standards to which the performance of job duties should conform is MOST often

    A. the work of the people responsible for seeing that the duties are properly performed
    B. accomplished by the person who is best informed about the functions involved
    C. the responsibility of the people who are to apply them
    D. attributable to the efforts of various informed persons

24. According to the above paragraph, when standards call for finer tolerances than those essential to the conduct of successful production operations, the effect of the standards on the improvement of production operations is

    A. negative   B. negligible
    C. nullified   D. beneficial

25. The one of the following which is the MOST suitable title for the above paragraph is

    A. THE EVALUATION OF FORMULATED STANDARDS
    B. THE ATTRIBUTES OF SATISFACTORY STANDARDS
    C. THE ADOPTION OF ACCEPTABLE STANDARDS
    D. THE USE OF PROCESS OR PRODUCT STANDARDS

KEY (CORRECT ANSWERS)

1.	B	11.	D
2.	A	12.	C
3.	E	13.	B
4.	D	14.	A
5.	E	15.	C
6.	C	16.	B
7.	A	17.	C
8.	D	18.	C
9.	A	19.	B
10.	C	20.	A

21. D
22. C
23. D
24. A
25. B

———

ENGLISH EXPRESSION
EXAMINATION SECTION
TEST 1

DIRECTIONS: Each question or incomplete statement is followed by several suggested answers or completions. Select the one that BEST answers the question or completes the statement. *PRINT THE LETTER OF THE CORRECT ANSWER IN THE SPACE AT THE RIGHT.*

Questions 1-9.

DIRECTIONS: The following sentences contain problems in grammar, usage diction (choice of words), and idiom. Some sentences are correct. No sentence contains more than one error. You will find that the error, if there is one, is underlined and lettered. Assume that all other elements of the sentence are correct and cannot be changed. In choosing answers, follow the requirements of standard written English. If there is an error, select the *one underlined* part that must be changed in order to make the sentence correct. If there is no error, mark E.

1. <u>In planning</u> your future, <u>one must be</u> as honest with yourself as possible, make careful
       A   B
   decisions about the best course <u>to follow to achieve</u> a particular purpose, and, above all,
                                            C
   have the courage <u>to stand by those</u> decisions. <u>No error</u>
                     D   E
   1.____

2. <u>Even though</u> history does not actually repeat itself, knowledge <u>of</u> history <u>can give</u>
       A   B   C
   current problems a familiar, <u>less</u> formidable look. <u>No error</u>
                          D   E
   2.____

3. The Curies <u>had almost exhausted</u> their resources, and <u>for a time it seemed</u>
                     A   B
   <u>unlikely that they ever</u> would find the <u>solvent to their financial problems</u>. <u>No error</u>
           C   D   E
   3.____

4. <u>If the rumors are</u> correct, Deane <u>will not be convicted</u>, for each of the officers
          A   B
   on the court realizes that Colson and Holdman may be <u>the real culprit and</u> that
                                                                  C
   <u>their</u> testimony is not completely trustworthy. <u>No error</u>
    D   E
   4.____

5. The citizens of Washington, <u>like Los Angeles</u>, prefer to commute by automobile,
          A
even though motor vehicles contribute <u>nearly as many</u> contaminants to the air
                                              B
<u>as do all other</u> sources <u>combined</u>. <u>No error</u>
        C   D   E

6. <u>By the time Robert Vasco completes</u> his testimony, every major executive of our
                       A
company but Ray Ashurst <u>and I</u> <u>will have been</u> <u>accused of</u> complicity in the stock
                          B   C   D
swindle. <u>No error</u>
              E

7. <u>Within six months</u> the store was operating <u>profitably and efficient</u>; shelves
         A   B
<u>were well stocked</u>, goods were selling rapidly, and the cash register
        C
<u>was ringing constantly</u>. <u>No error</u>
          D   E

8. Shakespeare's comedies have an advantage <u>over Shaw</u> <u>in that Shakespeare's</u> were
                                                  A   B
<u>written primarily</u> to entertain and <u>not to</u> argue for a cause. <u>No error</u>
        C   D   E

9. Any true insomniac <u>is well aware of</u> the futility of <u>such measures as</u> drinking
                              A   B
hot milk, <u>regular hours, deep breathing</u>, counting sheep, and <u>concentrating on</u>
                         C   D
black velvet. <u>No error</u>
                    E

Questions 10-15.

DIRECTIONS: In each of the following sentences, some part of the sentence or the entire sentence is underlined. Beneath each sentence you will find five ways of phrasing the underlined part. The first of these repeats the original; the other four are different. If you think the original is better than any of the alternatives, choose answer A; otherwise choose one of the others. In choosing answers, follow the requirements of standard written English; that is, pay attention to grammar, choice of words, sentence construction, and punctuation. Choose the answer that produces the most effective sentence—clear and exact, without awkwardness or ambiguity. Do not make a choice that changes the meaning of the original sentence.

10. The tribe of warriors believed that boys and girls should be <u>reared separate, and, as soon as he was weaned, the boys were taken from their mothers.</u>
    A. reared separate, and, as soon as he was weaned, the boys were taken from their mothers

B. reared separate, and, as soon as he was weaned, a boy was taken from his mother
C. reared separate, and, as soon as he was weaned, the boys were taken from their mothers
D. reared separately, and, as soon as a boy was weaned, they were taken from their mothers
E. reared separately, and, as soon as a boy was weaned, he was taken from his mother

11. <u>Despite Vesta being only the third largest, it is by far the brightest of the known asteroids.</u>
    A. Despite Vesta being only the third largest, it is by far the brightest of the known asteroids.
    B. Vesta, though only the third largest asteroid, is by far the brightest of the known ones.
    C. Being only the third largest, yet Vesta is by far the brightest of the known asteroids.
    D. Vesta, though only the third largest of the known asteroids, is by far the brightest.
    E. Vesta is only the third largest of the asteroids, it being, however, the brightest one.

12. As a result of the discovery of the Dead Sea Scrolls, our understanding of the roots of Christianity <u>has had to be revised considerably.</u>
    A. has had to be revised considerably
    B. have had to be revised considerably
    C. has had to undergo revision to a considerable degree
    D. have had to be subjected to considerable revision
    E. has had to be revised in a considerable way

13. Because <u>it is imminently suitable to</u> dry climates, adobe has been a traditional building material throughout the southwestern states.
    A. it is imminently suitable to
    B. it is eminently suitable for
    C. It is eminently suitable when in
    D. of its eminent suitability with
    E. of being imminently suitable in

14. <u>Martell is more concerned with demonstrating that racial prejudice exists than preventing it from doing harm, which explains</u> why his work is not always highly regarded.
    A. Martell is more concerned with demonstrating that racial prejudice exists than preventing it from doing harm, which explains
    B. Martell is more concerned with demonstrating that racial prejudice exists than with preventing it from doing harm, and this explains
    C. Martell is more concerned with demonstrating that racial prejudice exists than with preventing it from doing harm, an explanation of
    D. Martell's greater concern for demonstrating that racial prejudice exists than preventing it from doing harm—this explains
    E. Martell's greater concern for demonstrating that racial prejudice exists than for preventing it from doing harm explains

15. <u>Throughout this history of the American West there runs a steady commentary on the deception and mistreatment of the Indians.</u> 15.____
    A. Throughout this history of the American West there runs a steady commentary on the deception and mistreatment of the Indians.
    B. There is a steady commentary provided on the deception and mistreatment of the Indians and it runs throughout this history of the American West.
    C. The deception and mistreatment of the Indians provide a steady comment that runs throughout this history of the American West.
    D. Comment on the deception and mistreatment of the Indians is steadily provided and runs throughout this history of the American West.
    E. Running throughout this history of the American West is a steady commentary that is provided on the deception and mistreatment of the Indians.

Questions 16-20.

DIRECTIONS: In each of the following questions you are given a complete sentence to be rephrased according to the directions which follow it. You should rephrase the sentence mentally to save time, although you may make notes in your test book if you wish. Below each sentence and its directions are listed words or phrases that may occur in your revised sentence. When you have thought out a good sentence, look in the choices A through E for the word or entire phrase that is included in your revised sentence, and print the letter of the correct answer in the space at the right. The word or phrase you choose should be the most accurate and most nearly complete of all the choices given, and should be part of a sentence that meets the requirements of standard written English. Of course, a number of different sentences can be obtained if the sentence is revised according to directions, and not all of these possibilities can be included in only five choices. If you should find that you have thought of a sentence that contains none of the words or phrases listed in the choices, you should attempt to rephrase the sentence again so that it includes a word or phrase that is listed. Although the directions may at times require you to change the relationship between parts of the sentence or to make slight changes in meaning in other ways, <u>make only those changes that the directions require</u>; that is, keep the meaning the same, or as nearly the same as the directions permit. If you think that more than one good sentence can be made according to the directions, select the sentence that is most exact, effective, and natural in phrasing and construction.

EXAMPLES

I. <u>Sentence</u>: Coming to the city as a young man, he found a job as a newspaper reporter.
   <u>Directions</u>: Substitute <u>He came</u> for <u>Coming</u>.
   A. and so he found   B. and found
   C. and there he had found D. and then finding
   E. and had found

Your rephrased sentence will probably read: "He came to the city as a young man and found a job as a newspaper reporter." This sentence contains the correct answer: <u>B. and found</u>. A sentence which used one of the alternate phrases would <u>change the</u> meaning or <u>intention</u> of the original sentence, would be a <u>poorly written sentence</u>, or would be <u>less effective</u> than another possible revision.

II. <u>Sentence</u>: Owing to her wealth, Sarah had many suitors.
   <u>Directions</u>: Begin with <u>Many men courted</u>.
   A. so   B. while   C. although   D. because   E. and

Your rephrased sentence will probably read: "Many men courted Sarah because she was wealthy." This new sentence contains only choice D, which is the correct answer. None of the other choices will fit into an effective, correct sentence that retains the original meaning.

16. The archaeologists could only mark out the burial site, for then winter came.
    Begin with <u>Winter came before</u>.
    A. could do nothing more   B. could not do anything
    C. could only do   D. could do something
    E. could do anything more

17. The white reader often receives some insight into the reasons why black men are angry from descriptions by a black writer of the injustice they encounter in a white society.
    Begin with <u>A black writer often gives</u>.
    A. when describing   B. by describing
    C. he has described   D. in the descriptions
    E. because of describing

18. The agreement between the university officials and the dissident students provides for student representation on every university committee and on the board of trustees.
    Substitute <u>provides that</u> for <u>provides for</u>.
    A. be   B. are   C. would have
    D. would be   E. Is to be

19. English Romanticism had its roots in German idealist philosophy, first described in England by Samuel Coleridge.
    Begin with <u>Samuel Coleridge was the first in</u>.
    A. in which English   B. and from it English
    C. where English   D. the source of English
    E. the birth of English

20. Four months have passed since his dismissal, during which time Alan has looked for work daily.
    Begin with <u>Each day</u>.
    A. will have passed   B. that have passed   C. that passed
    D. were to pass   E. had passed

KEY (CORRECT ANSWERS)

1.	B	11.	D
2.	E	12.	A
3.	D	13.	B
4.	C	14.	E
5.	A	15.	A
6.	B	16.	E
7.	B	17.	B
8.	A	18.	A
9.	C	19.	D
10.	E	20.	B

WRITTEN ENGLISH EXPRESSION
EXAMINATION SECTION
TEST 1

DIRECTIONS: In each of the sentences below, four portions are underlined and lettered. Read each sentence and decide whether any of the UNDERLINED parts contains an error in spelling, punctuation, or capitalization, or employs grammatical usage which would be inappropriate for carefully written English. If so, note the letter printed under the unacceptable form and indicate this choice in the space at the right. If all four of the underlined portions are acceptable as they stand, select the answer E. (No sentence contains more than ONE unacceptable form.)

1. The revised <u>procedure</u> was <u>quite</u> different <u>than</u> the one which <u>was</u> employed up
                  A   B   C   D
to that time. <u>No error</u>
              E

1.____

2. <u>Blinded</u> by the storm that <u>surrounded</u> him, his plane <u>kept going</u> in <u>circles</u>.
    A   B   C   D
<u>No error</u>
  E

2.____

3. They <u>should</u> give the book to <u>whoever</u> <u>they</u> think deserves <u>it</u>. <u>No error</u>
        A   B   C   D E

3.____

4. The <u>government</u> will not consent to your <u>firm</u> <u>sending</u> that package as
       A   B   C
<u>second class</u> matter. <u>No error</u>
    D   E

4.____

5. She <u>would have</u> avoided all the trouble <u>that</u> followed if she <u>would have</u> waited
        A   B   C
ten minutes <u>longer</u>. <u>No error</u>
        D   E

5.____

6. <u>His</u> poetry, <u>when</u> it was carefully examined, showed <u>characteristics</u> not unlike
   A   B   C
<u>Wordsworth</u>. <u>No error</u>
    D   E

6.____

7. <u>In my opinion</u>, based upon long years of research, <u>I think</u> the plan offered by
      A   B
my opponent is <u>unsound</u>, because it is not <u>founded</u> on true facts. <u>No error</u>
            C   D   E

7.____

8. The soldiers of <u>Washington's</u> army at Valley Forge <u>were</u> men ragged in
                     A   B
   <u>appearance</u> but <u>who were</u> noble in character. <u>No error</u>
     C   D   E

9. Rabbits <u>have a distrust</u> of man <u>due to</u> the fact <u>that</u> they are <u>so often</u> shot.
              A   B   C   D
   <u>No error</u>
     E

10. <u>This</u> is the man <u>who</u> I believe <u>is</u> best <u>qualified</u> for the position. <u>No error</u>
      A   B   C   D   E

11. Her voice was <u>not only good</u>, but <u>she</u> also very clearly <u>enunciated</u>.
                   A   B   C   D
    <u>No error</u>
      E

12. <u>Today he</u> is wearing a <u>different</u> suit <u>than</u> the <u>one</u> he wore yesterday. <u>No error</u>
        A   B   C   D   E

13. Our work <u>is</u> to improve the club; if anybody <u>must</u> resign, let it <u>not</u> be you or <u>I</u>.
             A   B   C   D
    <u>No error</u>
      E

14. There was so much talking <u>in back of</u> me <u>as</u> I <u>could</u> not <u>enjoy</u> the music.
                                       A   B   C   D
    <u>No error</u>
      E

15. <u>Being that</u> he is that <u>kind of boy</u>, he cannot be blamed <u>for</u> the mistake.
        A   B   C   D
    <u>No error</u>
      E

16. <u>The king, having read</u> the speech, <u>he</u> and the <u>queen</u> <u>departed</u>. <u>No error</u>
                   A   B   C   D   E

17. I <u>am</u> <u>so tired</u> I <u>can't</u> <u>scarcely</u> stand. <u>No error</u>
      A   B   C   D   E

18. We are <u>mailing bills</u> to our customers <u>in Canada</u>, and, <u>being</u> eager to
                 A   B   C
    clear our books before the new season opens, it is <u>to be hoped</u> they will
                                                                      D
    send their remittances promptly. <u>No error</u>
                                        E

19. I reluctantly acquiesced to the proposal. No error   19.____
    A   B   C   D   E

20. It had lain out in the rain all night. No error   20.____
    A   B   C   D   E

21. If he would have gone there, he would have seen a marvelous sight.   21.____
          A   B   C   D
    No error
       E

22. The climate of Asia Minor is somewhat like Utah. No error   22.____
                  A   B   C   D   E

23. If everybody did unto others as they would wish others to do unto them, this   23.____
         A   B   C   D
    world would be a paradise. No error
                                   E

24. This was the jockey whom I saw was most likely to win the race. No error   24.____
    A   B   C   D   E

25. The only food the general demanded was potatoes. No error   25.____
         A   B   C   D   E

KEY (CORRECT ANSWERS)

1.	C	11.	C
2.	A	12.	C
3.	B	13.	D
4.	B	14.	B
5.	C	15.	A
6.	D	16.	A
7.	B	17.	C
8.	D	18.	C
9.	B	19.	E
10.	E	20.	E

21. A
22. D
23. D
24. B
25. E

TEST 2

DIRECTIONS: In each of the sentences below, four portions are underlined and lettered. Read each sentence and decide whether any of the UNDERLINED parts contains an error in spelling, punctuation, or capitalization, or employs grammatical usage which would be inappropriate for carefully written English. If so, note the letter printed under the unacceptable form and indicate this choice in the space at the right. If all four of the underlined portions are acceptable as they stand, select the answer E. (No sentence contains more than ONE unacceptable form.)

1. A party <u>like</u> <u>that</u> <u>only</u> <u>comes</u> once a year. <u>No error</u> 1.____
        A   B   C   D   E

2. <u>Our's</u> <u>is</u> <u>a</u> <u>swift moving</u> age. <u>No error</u> 2.____
    A   B C   D   E

3. The <u>healthy</u> climate soon <u>restored</u> him <u>to</u> his <u>accustomed</u> vigor. <u>No error</u> 3.____
      A   B   C   D   E

4. <u>They</u> needed six typists and hoped that <u>only</u> that <u>many</u> <u>would</u> apply for the position. <u>No error</u> 4.____
    A   B   C   D
                E

5. He <u>interviewed</u> people <u>whom</u> he thought had <u>something</u> <u>to impart</u>. <u>No error</u> 5.____
         A   B   C   D   E

6. <u>Neither</u> of his three sisters <u>is</u> older <u>than</u> <u>he</u>. <u>No error</u> 6.____
    A   B   C D   E

7. <u>Since</u> he is <u>that</u> kind <u>of</u> <u>a</u> boy, he cannot be expected to cooperate with us. <u>No error</u> 7.____
    A   B   C   D
   E

8. <u>When passing</u> <u>through</u> the tunnel, the air pressure <u>affected</u> <u>our</u> years. <u>No error</u> 8.____
      A   B   C   D   E

9. <u>The story having</u> a sad ending, <u>it</u> never <u>achieved</u> popularity <u>among</u> the students. <u>No error</u> 9.____
        A   B   C   D
              E

10. <u>Since</u> we are both hungry, <u>shall</u> we go <u>somewhere</u> for lunch? <u>No error</u> 10.____
     A   B   C   D   E

11. Will you please bring this book down to the library and give it to my friend, who is waiting for it? No error
    A   B   C   D
                                                                                                E

12. You may have the book; I am finished with it. No error
        A   B   C   D   E

13. I don't know if I should mention it to her or not. No error
      A   B   C   D   E

14. Philosophy is not a subject which has to do with philosophers and mathematics only. No error
                     A   B   C   D   E

15. The thoughts of the scholar in his library are little different than the old woman who first said, "It's no use crying over spilt milk." No error
                                 A   B
                                         C   D   E

16. A complete system of philosophical ideas are implied in many simple utterances. No error
                 A   B   C   D   E

17. Even if one has never put them into words, his ideas compose a kind of a philosophy. No error
         A   B   C   D
                                                                            E

18. Perhaps it is well enough that most people do not attempt this formulation. No error
            A B   C   D
    E

19. Leading their ordered lives, this confused body of ideas and feelings is sufficient. No error
        A   B   C   D
                E

20. Why should we insist upon them formulating it? No error
          A   B   C   D   E

21. Since it includes something of the wisdom of the ages, it is adequate for the purposes of ordinary life. No error
        A   B   C
            D   E

22. Therefore, I <u>have sought</u> to make a pattern <u>of mine,</u> <u>and so</u> there were, early
                          A   B   C
    moments of <u>my trying</u> to find out what were the elements with which I had to
                  D
    deal. <u>No error</u>
           E

    22.____

23. I <u>wanted</u> <u>to get</u> <u>what</u> knowledge I <u>could</u> about the general structure of the
        A   B   C   D
    universe. <u>No error</u>
               E

    23.____

24. I wanted to <u>know</u> <u>if</u> life <u>per se</u> had any meaning or <u>whether</u> I must strive to give
                 A B   C   D
    it one. <u>No error</u>
            E

    24.____

25. <u>So,</u> in a <u>desultory</u> way, I <u>began</u> <u>to read</u>. <u>No error</u>
     A   B   C   D   E

    25.____

KEY (CORRECT ANSWERS)

1.	C		11.	B
2.	A		12.	C
3.	A		13.	B
4.	C		14.	D
5.	B		15.	B
6.	A		16.	B
7.	D		17.	A
8.	A		18.	C
9.	A		19.	A
10.	E		20.	D

21.	E
22.	C
23.	C
24.	B
25.	E

WRITTEN ENGLISH EXPRESSION
EXAMINATION SECTION
TEST 1

DIRECTIONS: In each of the following groups of sentences, one of the four sentences is faulty in grammar, punctuation, or capitalization. Select the INCORRECT sentence in each case. *PRINT THE LETTER OF THE CORRECT ANSWER IN THE SPACE AT THE RIGHT.*

1. A. If you had stood at home and done your homework, you would not have failed in arithmetic.
   B. Her affected manner annoyed every member of the audience.
   C. How will the new law affect our income taxes?
   D. The plants were not affected by the long, cold winter, but they succumbed to the drought of summer.

   1.____

2. A. He is one of the most able men who have been in the Senate.
   B. It is he who is to blame for the lamentable mistake.
   C. Haven't you a helpful suggestion to make at this time?
   D. The money was robbed from the blind man's cup.

   2.____

3. A. The amount of children in this school is steadily increasing.
   B. After taking an apple from the table, she went out to play.
   C. He borrowed a dollar from me.
   D. I had hoped my brother would arrive before me.

   3.____

4. A. Whom do you think I hear from every week?
   B. Who do you think is the right man for the job?
   C. Who do you think I found in the room?
   D. He is the man whom we considered a good candidate for the presidency.

   4.____

5. A. Quietly the puppy laid down before the fireplace.
   B. You have made your bed; now lie in it.
   C. I was badly sunburned because I had lain too long in the sun.
   D. I laid the doll on the bed and left the room.

   5.____

6. A. Sailing down the bay was a thrilling experience for me.
   B. He was not consulted about your joining the club.
   C. This story is different than the one I told you yesterday.
   D. There is no doubt about his being the best player.

   6.____

7. A. He maintains there is but one road to world peace.
    B. It is common knowledge that a child sees much he is not supposed to see.
    C. Much of the bitterness might have been avoided if arbitration had been restored to earlier in the meeting.
    D. The man decided it would be advisable to marry a girl somewhat younger than him.

    7._____

8. A. In this book, the incident I liked least is where the hero tries to put out the forest fire.
    B. Learning a foreign language will undoubtedly give a person a better understanding of his mother tongue.
    C. His actions made us wonder what he planned to do next.
    D. Because of the war, we were unable to travel during the summer vacation.

    8._____

9. A. The class had no sooner become interested in the lesson than the dismissal bell rang.
    B. There is little agreement about the kind of world to be planned at the peace conference.
    C. "Today," said the teacher, "we shall read 'The Wind in the Willows.' I am sure you'll like it."
    D. The terms of the legal settlement of the family quarrel handicapped both sides for many years.

    9._____

10. A. I was so surprised that I was not able to say a word.
    B. She is taller than any other member of the class.
    C. It would be much more preferable if you were never seen in his company.
    D. We had no choice but to excuse her for being late.

    10._____

KEY (CORRECT ANSWERS)

1.	A	6.	C
2.	D	7.	D
3.	A	8.	A
4.	C	9.	C
5.	A	10.	C

TEST 2

DIRECTIONS: In each of the following groups of sentences, one of the four sentences is faulty in grammar, punctuation, or capitalization. Select the INCORRECT sentence in each case. *PRINT THE LETTER OF THE CORRECT ANSWER IN THE SPACE AT THE RIGHT.*

1. A. Please send me these data at the earliest opportunity.
    B. The loss of their material proved to be a severe handicap.
    C. My principal objection to this plan is that it is impracticable.
    D. The doll had laid in the rain for an hour and was ruined.

    1._____

2. A. The garden scissors, left out all night in the rain, were in a badly rusted condition.
    B. The girls felt bad about the misunderstanding which had arisen.
    C. Sitting near the campfire, the old man told John and I about many exciting adventures he had had.
    D. Neither of us is in a position to undertake a task of that magnitude.

    2._____

3. A. The general concluded that one of the three roads would lead to the besieged city.
    B. The children didn't, as a rule, do hardly anything beyond what they were told to do.
    C. The reason the girl gave for her negligence was that she had acted on the spur of the moment.
    D. The daffodils and tulips look beautiful in that blue vase.

    3._____

4. A. If I was ten years older, I should be interested in this work.
    B. Give the prize to whoever has drawn the best picture.
    C. When you have finished reading the book, take it back to the library.
    D. My drawing is as good as or better than yours.

    4._____

5. A. He asked me whether the substance was animal or vegetable.
    B. An apple which is unripe should not be eaten by a child.
    C. That was an insult to me who am your friend.
    D. Some spy must of reported the matter to the enemy.

    5._____

6. A. Limited time makes quoting the entire message impossible.
    B. Who did she say was going?
    C. The girls in your class have dressed more dolls this year than we.
    D. There was such a large amount of books on the floor that I couldn't find a place for my rocking chair.

    6._____

7. A. What with his sleeplessness and his ill health, he was unable to assume any responsibility for the success of the meeting.
    B. If I had been born in February, I should be celebrating my birthday soon.
    C. In order to prevent breakage, she placed a sheet of paper between each of the plates when she packed them.
    D. After the spring shower, the violets smelled very sweet.

    7._____

2 (#2)

8. A. He had laid the book down very reluctantly before the end of the lesson. 8.____
    B. The dog, I am sorry to say, had lain on the bed all night.
    C. The cloth was first lain on a flat surface; then it was pressed with a hot iron.
    D. While we were in Florida, we lay in the sun until we were noticeably tanned.

9. A. If John was in New York during the recent holiday season, I have no doubt 9.____
       he spent most of time with his parents.
    B. How could he enjoy the television program; the dog was barking and the
       baby was crying.
    C. When the problem was explained to the class, he must have been asleep.
    D. She wished that her new dress were finished so that she could go to the
       party.

10. A. The engine not only furnishes power but light and heat as well. 10.____
    B. You're aware that we've forgotten whose guilt was established, aren't you?
    C. Everybody knows that the woman made many sacrifices for her children.
    D. A man with his dog and gun is a familiar sight in this neighborhood.

KEY (CORRECT ANSWERS)

1. D 6. D
2. C 7. B
3. B 8. C
4. A 9. B
5. D 10. A

TEST 3

DIRECTIONS: Each of sentences 1 through 18 may be classified most appropriately under one of the following three categories:
- A. faulty because of incorrect grammar
- B. faulty because of incorrect punctuation
- C. correct

Examine each sentence carefully. Then, in the space at the right, print the capital letter preceding the option which is BEST of the three suggested above. All incorrect sentences contain but one type of error. Consider a sentence correct if it contains none of the types of errors mentioned, even though there may be other correct ways of expressing the same thought.

1. He sent the notice to the clerk who you hired yesterday. 1.____

2. It must be admitted, however that you were not informed of this change. 2.____

3. Only the employees who have served in this grade for at least two years are eligible for promotion. 3.____

4. The work was divided equally between she and Mary. 4.____

5. He thought that you were not available at that time. 5.____

6. When the messenger returns; please give him this package. 6.____

7. The new secretary prepared, typed, addressed, and delivered, the notices. 7.____

8. Walking into the room, his desk can be seen at the rear. 8.____

9. Although John has worked here longer than she, he produces a smaller amount of work. 9.____

10. She said she could of typed this report yesterday. 10.____

11. Neither one of these procedures are adequate for the efficient performance of this task. 11.____

12. The typewriter is the tool of the typist; the cash register, the tool of the cashier. 12.____

13. "The assignment must be completed as soon as possible" said the supervisor. 13.____

14. As you know, office handbooks are issued to all new employees. 14.____

15. Writing a speech is sometimes easier than to deliver it before an audience. 15.____

81

16. Mr. Brown, our accountant, will audit the accounts next week. 16.____

17. Give the assignment to whomever is able to do it most efficiently. 17.____

18. The supervisor expected either your or I to file these reports. 18.____

KEY (CORRECT ANSWERS)

1.	A	11.	A
2.	B	12.	C
3.	C	13.	B
4.	A	14.	C
5.	C	15.	A
6.	B	16.	B
7.	B	17.	A
8.	A	18.	A
9.	C		
10.	A		

TEST 4

DIRECTIONS: Each sentence may be classified most appropriately under one of the following four categories:
- A. faulty because of incorrect grammar
- B. faulty because of incorrect punctuation
- C. faulty because of incorrect spelling
- D. correct

Examine each sentence carefully. Then, in the space at the right, print the capital letter preceding the BEST of the four suggested above. All incorrect sentences contain but one type of error. Consider a sentence correct if it contains none of the types of errors mentioned, even though there may be other correct ways of expressing the same thought.

1. The fire apparently started in the storeroom, which is usually locked. 1.____
2. On approaching the victim two bruises were noticed by this officer. 2.____
3. The officer, who was there examined the report with great care. 3.____
4. Each employee in the office had a seperate desk. 4.____
5. All employees including members of the clerical staff, were invited to the lecture. 5.____
6. The suggested procedure is similar to the one now in use. 6.____
7. No one was more pleased with the new procedure than the chauffeur. 7.____
8. He tried to pursuade her to change the procedure. 8.____
9. The total of the expenses charged to petty cash were high. 9.____
10. An understanding between him and I was finally reached. 10.____

KEY (CORRECT ANSWERS)

1.	D	6.	D
2.	A	7.	D
3.	B	8.	C
4.	C	9.	A
5.	B	10.	A

TEST 5

Questions 1-5.

DIRECTIONS: Each of sentences 1 to 5 may be classified under one of the following four categories:
    A. faulty because of incorrect grammar
    B. faulty because of incorrect punctuation
    C. faulty because of incorrect capitalization or incorrect spelling
    D. correct

Examine each sentence carefully to determine under which of the above four options it is best classified. Then, in the space at the right, print the capital letter preceding the option which is the BEST of the four suggested above. Each faulty sentence contains but one type of error. Consider a sentence to be correct if it contains none of the types of errors mentioned, even though there may be other correct ways of expressing the same thought.

1. They told both he and I that the prisoner had escaped.   1.____

2. Any superior officer, who, disregards the just complaints of his subordinates, is remiss in the performance of his duty.   2.____

3. Only those members of the National organization who resided in the Middle West attended the conference in Chicago.   3.____

4. We told him to give the investigation assignment to whoever was available.   4.____

5. Please do not disappoint and embarass us by not appearing in court.   5.____

Questions 6-10.

DIRECTIONS: Each of questions 6 through 10 consists of a sentence. Read each sentence carefully and then write your answer to each question according to the following scheme:
    A. Sentence contains an error in spelling only
    B. Sentence contains an error in grammar or word usage only
    C. Sentence contains one error in spelling and one error in grammar or word usage
    D. Sentence is correct; contains no errors

6. Although the officer's speech proved to be entertaining, the topic was not relevant to the main theme of the conference.   6.____

7. In February all new officers attended a training course in which they were learned their principal duties and the fundamental operating procedures of the department.   7.____

8. I personally seen inmate Jones threaten inmates Smith and Green with bodily harm if they refused to participate in the plot. 8.____

9. To the layman, who on a chance visit to the prison observes everything functioning smoothly, the maintenance of prison discipline may seem to be a relatively easily realizable objective. 9.____

10. The prisoners in cell block fourty were forbidden to lay on the cell cots during the recreation hour. 10.____

KEY (CORRECT ANSWERS)

1.	A	6.	D
2.	B	7.	C
3.	C	8.	B
4.	D	9.	D
5.	C	10.	C

TEST 6

DIRECTIONS: Each of the following sentences may be classified under one of the following four categories:
- A. faulty because of incorrect grammar
- B. faulty because of incorrect punctuation
- C. faulty because of incorrect capitalization or incorrect spelling
- D. correct

Examine each sentence carefully to determine under which of the above four options it is best classified. Then, in the space at the right, print the capital letter preceding the option which is the BEST of the four suggested above. Each faulty sentence contains but one type of error. Consider a sentence to be correct if it contains none of the types of errors mentioned, even though there may be other correct ways of expressing the same thought.

1. I cannot encourage you any.   1._____
2. You always look well in those sort of clothes.   2._____
3. Shall we go to the park?   3._____
4. The man whome he introduced was Mr. Carey.   4._____
5. She saw the letter laying here this morning.   5._____
6. It should rain before the Afternoon is over.   6._____
7. They have already went home.   7._____
8. That Jackson will be elected is evident.   8._____
9. He does not hardly approve of us.   9._____
10. It was he, who won the prize.   10._____

KEY (CORRECT ANSWERS)

1.	A	6.	C
2.	A	7.	A
3.	D	8.	D
4.	C	9.	A
5.	A	10.	B

TEST 7

DIRECTIONS: Each of the following sentences may be classified under one of the following four categories:
- A. faulty because of incorrect grammar
- B. faulty because of incorrect punctuation
- C. faulty because of incorrect capitalization or incorrect spelling
- D. correct

Examine each sentence carefully to determine under which of the above four options it is best classified. Then, in the space at the right, print the capital letter preceding the option which is the BEST of the four suggested above. Each faulty sentence contains but one type of error. Consider a sentence to be correct if it contains none of the types of errors mentioned, even though there may be other correct ways of expressing the same thought.

1. Shall we go to the park.   1.____
2. They are, alike, in this particular.   2.____
3. They gave the poor man sume food when he knocked on the door.   3.____
4. I regret the loss caused by the error.   4.____
5. The students' will have a new teacher.   5.____
6. They sweared to bring out all the facts.   6.____
7. He decided to open a branch store on 33rd street.   7.____
8. His speed is equal and more than that of a racehorse.   8.____
9. He felt very warm on that Summer day.   9.____
10. He was assisted by his friend, who lives in the next house.   10.____

KEY (CORRECT ANSWERS)

1. B
2. B
3. C
4. D
5. B
6. A
7. C
8. A
9. C
10. D

TEST 8

DIRECTIONS: Each of the following sentences may be classified under one of the following four categories:
- A. faulty because of incorrect grammar
- B. faulty because of incorrect punctuation
- C. faulty because of incorrect capitalization or incorrect spelling
- D. correct

Examine each sentence carefully to determine under which of the above four options it is best classified. Then, in the space at the right, print the capital letter preceding the option which is the BEST of the four suggested above. Each faulty sentence contains but one type of error. Consider a sentence to be correct if it contains none of the types of errors mentioned, even though there may be other correct ways of expressing the same thought.

1. The climate of New York is colder than California. 1.____

2. I shall wait for you on the corner. 2.____

3. Did we see the boy who, we think, is the leader. 3.____

4. Being a modest person, John seldom talks about his invention. 4.____

5. The gang is called the smith street boys. 5.____

6. He seen the man break into the store. 6.____

7. We expected to lay still there for quite a while. 7.____

8. He is considered to be the Leader of his organization. 8.____

9. Although I recieved an invitation, I won't go. 9.____

10. The letter must be here some place. 10.____

KEY (CORRECT ANSWERS)

1.	A	6.	A
2.	D	7.	A
3.	B	8.	C
4.	D	9.	C
5.	C	10.	A

TEST 9

DIRECTIONS: Each of the following sentences may be classified under one of the following four categories:
- A. faulty because of incorrect grammar
- B. faulty because of incorrect punctuation
- C. faulty because of incorrect capitalization or incorrect spelling
- D. correct

Examine each sentence carefully to determine under which of the above four options it is best classified. Then, in the space at the right, print the capital letter preceding the option which is the BEST of the four suggested above. Each faulty sentence contains but one type of error. Consider a sentence to be correct if it contains none of the types of errors mentioned, even though there may be other correct ways of expressing the same thought.

1. I thought it to be he. 1.____
2. We expect to remain here for a long time. 2.____
3. The committee was agreed. 3.____
4. Two-thirds of the building are finished. 4.____
5. The water was froze. 5.____
6. Everyone of the salesmen must supply their own car. 6.____
7. Who is the author of Gone With The Wind? 7.____
8. He marched on and declaring that he would never surrender. 8.____
9. Who shall I say called? 9.____
10. Everyone has left but they. 10.____

KEY (CORRECT ANSWERS)

1. A   6. A
2. D   7. B
3. A   8. A
4. A   9. D
5. A   10. D

TEST 10

DIRECTIONS: Each of the following sentences may be classified under one of the following four categories:
- A. faulty because of incorrect grammar
- B. faulty because of incorrect punctuation
- C. faulty because of incorrect capitalization or incorrect spelling
- D. correct

Examine each sentence carefully to determine under which of the above four options it is best classified. Then, in the space at the right, print the capital letter preceding the option which is the BEST of the four suggested above. Each faulty sentence contains but one type of error. Consider a sentence to be correct if it contains none of the types of errors mentioned, even though there may be other correct ways of expressing the same thought.

1. Who did we give the order to? 1.____
2. Send your order in immediately. 2.____
3. I believe I paid the Bill. 3.____
4. I have not met but one person. 4.____
5. Why aren't Tom, and Fred, going to the dance? 5.____
6. What reason is there for him not going? 6.____
7. The seige of Malta was a tremendous event. 7.____
8. I was there yesterday I assure you. 8.____
9. Your ukulele is better than mine. 9.____
10. No one was there only Mary. 10.____

KEY (CORRECT ANSWERS)

1.	A	6.	A
2.	D	7.	C
3.	C	8.	B
4.	A	9.	C
5.	B	10.	A

WRITTEN ENGLISH EXPRESSION
EXAMINATION SECTION
TEST 1

DIRECTIONS: The following questions are designed to test your knowledge of grammar, sentence structure, correct usage, and punctuation. In each group, there is one sentence that contains an error. Select the letter of the INCORRECT sentence. *PRINT THE LETTER OF THE CORRECT ANSWER IN THE SPACE AT THE RIGHT.*

1. A. All things considered, he did unusually well.
    B. The poor boy takes everything too seriously.
    C. Our club sent two delegates, Ruth and I, to Oswego.
    D. I like him better than her.
    E. His eccentricities continually made good newspaper copy.

    1.____

2. A. If we except Benton, no one in the club foresaw the changes.
    B. The two-year-old rosebushes are loaded with buds—and beetles!
    C. Though the pitcher had been broken by the cat, Teena was furious.
    D. Virginia got the cake recipe off of her grandmother.
    E. Neither one of the twins was able to get a summer vacation.

    2.____

3. A. "What do you wish?" he asked, "may I help you?"
    B. Whose gloves are these?
    C. Has he drink all the orange juice?
    D. It was he who spoke to the manager of the store.
    E. Mary prefers this kind of evening dress.

    3.____

4. A. Charles himself said it before the assembled peers of the realm.
    B. The wind stirred the rose petals laying on the floor.
    C. The storm beat hard on the frozen windowpanes.
    D. Worn out by the days of exposure and storm, the sailor clung pitifully to the puny raft.
    E. The day afterward he thought more kindly of the matter.

    4.____

5. A. Between you and me, I think Henry is wrong.
    B. This is the more interesting of the two books.
    C. This is the most carefully written letter of all.
    D. During the opening course I read not only four plays but also three historical novels.
    E. This assortment of candies, nuts, and fruits are excellent.

    5.____

6. A. According to your report card, you are not so clever as he.
    B. If he had kept his eyes open, he would not have fallen into that trap.
    C. We were certain that the horse had broken it's leg.
    D. The troop of scouts and the leader are headed for the North Woods.
    E. I knew it to be him by the knock at the door.

    6.____

7. A. Being one of the earliest spring flowers, we welcome the crocus. 7._____
    B. The cold running water became colder as time sped on.
    C. Those boys need not have stood in line for lunch.
    D. Can you, my friend, donate ten dollars to the cause?
    E. Because it's a borrowed umbrella, return it in the morning.

8. A. If Walter would have planted earlier in the spring, the rosebushes would 8._____
       have survived.
    B. The flowers smell overpoweringly sweet.
    C. There are three *e*'s in dependent.
    D. May I be excused at the end of the test?
    E. Carl has three brothers-in-law.

9. A. We have bought neither the lumber nor the tools for the job. 9._____
    B. Jefferson was re-elected despite certain powerful opposition.
    C. The Misses Jackson were invited to the dance.
    D. The letter is neither theirs nor yours.
    E. The retail price for those items are far beyond the wholesale quotations.

10. A. To find peace of mind is to gain treasure beyond price. 10._____
    B. Fred is cheerful, carefree; his brother is morose.
    C. Whoever fails to understand the strategic importance of the Arctic fails to
       understand modern geography.
    D. They came promptly at 8 o'clock on August 7, 2020, without prior
       notification.
    E. Every one tried their best to guess the answer, but no one succeeded.

11. A. Is this hers or theirs? 11._____
    B. Having been recognized, Frank took the floor.
    C. Alex invited Sue; Paul, Marion; and Dan, Helen.
    D. If I were able to do the task, you can be sure that I'd do it.
    E. Stamp collecting, or philately as it is otherwise called is truly an
       international hobby.

12. A. He has proved himself to be reliable. 12._____
    B. The fisherman had arisen before the sun.
    C. By the time the truck arrived, I had put out the blaze.
    D. The doctor with his colleagues were engaged in consultation.
    E. I chose to try out a new method, but in spite of my efforts it failed.

13. A. He has drunk too much iced tea. 13._____
    B. I appreciated him doing that job for me.
    C. The royal family fled, but they were retaken.
    D. The secretary and the treasurer were both present on Friday,
    E. Iago protested his honesty, yet he continued to plot against Desdemona.

14. A. The family were all together at Easter.
    B. It is altogether too fine a day for us to stay indoors.
    C. However much you dislike him, you should treat him fairly.
    D. The judges were already there when the contestants arrived.
    E. The boy's mother reported that he was alright again after the accident.

    14.____

15. A. Ham and eggs is a substantial breakfast.
    B. By the end of the week the pond had frozen.
    C. I should appreciate any assistance you could offer me.
    D. Being that tomorrow is Sunday, we expect to close early.
    E. If he were to win the medal, I for one would be disturbed.

    15.____

16. A. Give the letter to whoever comes for it.
    B. He feels bad, but his sister is the one who looks sicker.
    C. He had an unbelievable large capacity for hard physical work.
    D. Earth has nothing more beautiful to offer than the autumn colors of this section of the country.
    E. Happily we all have hopes that the future will soon bring forth fruits of a lasting peace.

    16.____

17. A. This kind of apples is my favorite.
    B. Either of the players is capable of performing ably.
    C. Though trying my best to be calm, the choice was not an easy one for me.
    D. The nearest star is not several light years away; it is only 93,000,000 miles away.
    E. There were two things I still wished to do—to see the Lincoln Memorial and to climb up the Washington Monument.

    17.____

18. A. It is I who is to blame.
    B. That dress looks very good on Jane.
    C. People often take my brother to be me.
    D. I could but think she had deceived me.
    E. He himself told us that the story was true,

    18.____

19. A. They all went but Mabel and me.
    B. Has he ever swum across the river?
    C. We have a dozen other suggestions besides these.
    D. The Jones's are going to visit their friends in Chicago.
    E. The ideal that Arthur and his knights were in quest of was a better world order.

    19.____

20. A. Would I were able to be there with you!
    B. Whomever he desires to see should be admitted.
    C. It is not for such as we to follow fashion blindly.
    D. His causing the confusion seemed to affect him not at all.
    E. Please notify all those whom you think should have this information.

    20.____

21. A. She was not only competent but also friendly in nature.
     B. Not only must we visualize the play we are reading; we must actually hear it.
     C. The firm was not only acquiring a bad reputation but also indulging in illegal practices.
     D. The bank was not only uncooperative but also was indifferent to new business offered them.
     E. I know that a conscious effort was made not only to guard the material but also to keep it from being used.

     21._____

22. A. How old shall you be on your next birthday?
     B. I am sure that he has been here and did what was expected of him.
     C. Near to the bank of the river, stood, secluded and still, the house of the hermit.
     D. Because of its efficacy in treating many ailments, penicillin has become an important addition to the druggist's stock.
     E. ROBINSON CRUSOE, which is a fairy tale to the child, is a work of social philosophy to the mature thinker.

     22._____

23. A. We had no sooner started than it rained.
     B. The fact that the prisoner is a minor will be taken into consideration.
     C. Many parents think more of their older children than of their younger ones.
     D. The boy laid a book, a knife and a fishing line on the table.
     E. John is the tallest of any boy in his class.

     23._____

24. A. Although we have been friend for many years, I must admit that May is most inconsiderate.
     B. He is not able to run, not even to walk.
     C. You will bear this pain as you have so many greater ones.
     D. The harder the work, the more studious she became.
     E. Too many "and's" in a sentence produce an immature style.

     24._____

25. A. It would be preferable to have you submit questions after, not before, the lecture.
     B. Plan your work; then work your plan.
     C. At last John met his brother, who had been waiting two hours for him.
     D. Should one penalize ones self for not trying?
     E. There are other considerations besides this one.

     25._____

KEY (CORRECT ANSWERS)

1.	C		11.	E
2.	D		12.	D
3.	A		13.	B
4.	B		14.	E
5.	E		15.	D
6.	C		16.	C
7.	A		17.	C
8.	A		18.	A
9.	E		19.	D
10.	E		20.	E

21. D
22. B
23. E
24. C
25. D

TEST 2

DIRECTIONS: The following questions are designed to test your knowledge of grammar, sentence structure, correct usage, and punctuation. In each group, there is one sentence that contains an error. Select the letter of the INCORRECT sentence. *PRINT THE LETTER OF THE CORRECT ANSWER IN THE SPACE AT THE RIGHT.*

1. A. "Halt!" cried the sentry, "Who goes there?"
    B. "It is in talk alone," said Robert Louis Stevenson, "that we can learn our period and ourselves."
    C. The world will long remember the "culture" of the Nazis.
    D. When duty says, "You must," the youth replies, "I can."
    E. Who said, "Give me liberty or give me death?"

1.____

2. A. Why are you so quiet, Martha?
    B. Edward Jones, a banker who lives near us, expects to retire very soon.
    C. I picked up the solid-gold chain.
    D. Any boy, who refuses to tell the truth, will be punished.
    E. Yes, honey tastes sweet.

2.____

3. A. I knew it to be him by the style of his clothes.
    B. No one saw him doing it.
    C. Her going away is a loss to the community.
    D. Mary objected to her being there.
    E. Illness prevented him graduating in June.

3.____

4. A. Being tired, I stretched out on a grassy knoll.
    B. While we were rowing on the lake, a sudden squall almost capsized the boat.
    C. Entering the room, a strange mark on the floor attracted my attention.
    D. Mounting the curb, the empty car crossed the sidewalk and came to rest against a building.
    E. Sitting down, they watched him demonstrate his skill.

4.____

5. A. The coming of peace effected a change in her way of life.
    B. Spain is as weak, if not weaker than, she was in 1900.
    C. In regard to that, I am not certain what my attitude will be.
    D. That unfortunate family faces the problem of adjusting itself to a new way of life.
    E. Fred Eastman states in his essay that one of the joys of reading lies in discovering courage.

5.____

6. A. Not one in a thousand readers take the matter seriously.
    B. Let it lie there.
    C. You are not as tall as he.
    D. The people began to realize how much she had done.
    E. He was able partially to accomplish his purpose.

6.____

2 (#2)

7. A. In the case of members who are absent, a special letter will be sent. 7.____
    B. The visitors were all ready to see it.
    C. I like Burns's poem "To a Mountain Daisy."
    D. John told William that he was sure he had seen it.
    E. Both men are Yale alumni.

8. A. The audience took their seats promptly. 8.____
    B. Each boy and girl must finish his examination this morning.
    C. Every person turned their eyes toward the door.
    D. Everyone has his own opinion.
    E. The club nominated its officers by secret ballot.

9. A. I can do that more easily than you. 9.____
    B. This kind of weather is more healthful.
    C. Pick out the really important points.
    D. Because of his aggressive nature, he only plays the hardest games.
    E. He pleaded with me to let him go.

10. A. It is I who am mistaken. 10.____
    B. Is it John or Susie who stand at the head of the class?
    C. He is one of those who always do their lessons.
    D. He is a man on whom I can depend in time of trouble.
    E. Had he known who it was, he would have come.

11. A. Somebody has forgotten his umbrella. 11.____
    B. Please let Joe and me use the car.
    C. We thought the author to be he.
    D. Whoever they send will be welcome.
    E. They thought the intruders were we.

12. A. If I had known that you were coming, I should have met you. 12.____
    B. All the girls but her were at the game.
    C. I expected to have heard the concert before the present time.
    D. Walter would not have said it if he had thought it would make her unhappy.
    E. I have always believed that cork is the best material for insulation.

13. A. Their contributions amounted to the no insignificant sum of ten thousand dollars. 13.____
    B. None of them was there.
    C. Ten dollars is the amount I agreed to pay.
    D. Fewer than one hundred persons assembled.
    E. Exactly what many others have done and are doing, Frank did.

14. A. Neither Jane or her sister has arrived. 14.____
    B. Either Richard or his brother is going to drive.
    C. Refilling storage batteries is the work of the youngest employee.
    D. Helen has to lie still for two weeks.
    E. Mother lay down for an hour yesterday.

15. A. He is not the man whom you saw entering the house.
    B. He asked why I wouldn't come.
    C. This is the cow whose horns are the longest.
    D. Helen, this is a man I met on the train one day last February.
    E. He greeted every foreign representative which came to the conference.

16. A. You, but not I, are invited.
    B. Guy's technique of service and return is masterly.
    C. Please pass me one of the books that are lying on the table.
    D. Mathematics is my most difficult subject.
    E. Unable to agree on a plan of organization, the class has departed in several directions.

17. A. He spoke to Gertrude and to me of the seriousness of the occasion.
    B. They seem to have decided to invite everyone except you and I.
    C. Your attitude is insulting to me who am your friend.
    D. He wished to know who our representative was.
    E. You may tell whomsoever you wish.

18. A. My favorite studies were Latin and science.
    B. The committee made its report.
    C. To get your work done promptly is better than leaving it until the last minute.
    D. That's what he would do if he were governor.
    E. He said that his chosen colors were red and blue.

19. A. Punish whoever disobeys orders.
    B. Come here, Henry; and sit with me.
    C. Has either of them his notebook?
    D. He talked as if he meant it.
    E. You did well; therefore you should be rewarded.

20. A. Many of us students were called to work.
    B. He shot the albatross with a crossbow.
    C. A house that is set on a hill is conspicuous.
    D. The wooden beams had raised slowly about a foot and then had settled back into place.
    E. Whom do you want to go with you?

21. A. He does not drive as he should.
    B. I can't hardly wait for the holidays.
    C. I like it less well than last week's.
    D. You were troubled by his coming.
    E. I don't know but that you are correct.

22. A. He was angry at both of us, her and me.
    B. When one enters the town, they see big crowds.
    C. They laid the tools on the ground every night.
    D. He is the only one of my friends who has written.
    E. He asked for a raise in wages.

23. A. None came with his excuse.
    B. Walking down the street, a house comes into view.
    C. "Never!" shouted the boy.
    D. Both are masters of their subject.
    E. His advice was to drive slowly.

    23._____

24. A. There is both beef and lamb on the market.
    B. Either beans or beets are enough with potatoes.
    C. Where does your mother buy bananas?
    D. Dinners at the new restaurant are excellent.
    E. Each was rewarded according to his deeds.

    24._____

25. A. Accordingly, we must prepare the food.
    B. The work, moreover, must be done today.
    C. Nevertheless, we must first have dinner.
    D. I always chose the most liveliest of the ponies.
    E. At six o'clock tomorrow the job will have been completed,

    25._____

KEY (CORRECT ANSWERS)

1.	E		11.	C
2.	D		12.	C
3.	E		13.	A
4.	C		14.	A
5.	B		15.	E
6.	A		16.	E
7.	C		17.	B
8.	C		18.	C
9.	D		19.	B
10.	B		20.	D

21.	B
22.	B
23.	B
24.	A
25.	D

TEST 3

DIRECTIONS: In each group of five sentences below, one or more sentences contain an error in usage. Choose the lettered answer which indicates ALL the sentences containing errors in usage. *PRINT THE LETTER OF THE CORRECT ANSWER IN THE SPACE AT THE RIGHT.*

1. I. Shortly after the terms of the contract for the new road transpired, an aroused constituency showed its disapproval by voting the senator out of office.
    II. Neither father nor sons work for a living but spend their days in drinking and gambling at the pub.
    III. Like his Italian predecessor, Boccaccio, whose DECAMERON was used as a model, a company of people of various occupations and stations in life, brought together for a pilgrimage, are called upon to relate stories to help relieve the tedium of their journey,
    IV. Sarah hurried into the kitchen and after a half hour emerged with a nauseous brew which she called coffee.
    V. It was to the major that the people applied for redress and by his armed guards that they were driven away.
    The CORRECT answer is:
    A. I B. III C. I, II, III D. IV, III E. II, III

    1.____

2. I. As we approached the castle, which was illuminated suddenly by the full moon breaking through the clouds, we described a rider coming to meet us.
    II. The reason for his loss of interest in boxing, as far as I can see, was due to the pressure of his work and the distance of the local "Y" from his home.
    III. Accompanied by a handsome member of the British legation, Elsie was about to enter the luxuriously furnished salon to meet the countess.
    IV. In spite of all of John's gifts and attentions, little Rosalie, upon being asked to make a choice, said she liked me better than him.
    V. The scar of the clearing for the power line extended for a hundred miles over the mountains, and the great poles with fifty feet between each carried cable from Niagara to Albany.
    The CORRECT answer is:
    A. II, III B. I, IV, III C. I, II, IV, III
    D. II, V E. III, V

    2.____

3. I. The high wind had blown the roofs of several houses; the water supply had been contaminated by the floods; transportation to the business center had ground to a half; but the mayor said there was no reason for alarm!
    II. Because there is a need to soften tragic or painful news, we resort to such euphuisms for the simple "to die" as "to pass away," "to go to a better world," or "to join the great majority."
    III. Hardly had the salient on the western shore of the river been obliterated than one on the eastern bank crossed on a pontoon bridge and in boats of all sorts.
    IV. The distinction between the man who gives in a spirit of charity and him who gives for social recognition is often to be seen in the nature of the gift.
    V. After a few months in office, the new superintendent effected many changes, not all of them for the good, in the administration of the plant.

    3.____

The CORRECT answer is:
A. II, III   B. II, III, IV   C. III, IV   D. I, II, V   E. I, II, III

4. I. The defendants published an advertisement and notice giving information, directly and indirectly, stating where, how, and when, and by what means and what purports to be the said book can be purchased.
    II. In common with most Eskimos of her time, she had long spells of silence; and nature, while endowing her with immense sagacity, had thrust on her a compelling reticence.
    III. The entire report was read in less than half an hour to the full committee, giving no time for comment or question, and offered for vote.
    IV. Students going through this course almost always find themselves becoming critical of their own writing.
    V. In his report of 1968, Mr. Jones states that his chief problem is the rapid turnover of personnel which has prevailed to the moment of writing.
    The CORRECT answer is:
    A. I, IV   B. II, III   C. III, IV, V   D. I, IV, V   E. I, III

5. I. The material was destroyed after it had served our purposes, and after portions of it had been excluded and portions included in our report.
    II. We checked our results very carefully, too carefully perhaps, for we spent several hours on our task.
    III. We should keep constantly in mind the fact that writing has no purpose save to meet the needs of the reader.
    IV. Not even discussed in October, when Lathrop flew in from the Coast, the problem of expense was settled at the June meeting.
    V. Whether our facts were right or not, it was not necessary for you to rebuke him in such a discourteous manner.
    The CORRECT answer is:
    A. I only   B. I, IV   C. II, III   D. V only   E. I, V

6. I. At first the novel was interesting and liked by members of the class; but later the long reading assignments dampened the pupils' enthusiasm.
    II. Donnie had no love or confidence in his mother, who, when abandoned by her husband, put the boy in an orphanage and seldom went to visit him.
    III. Built during the Civil War, the house has a delicate air, supported as it is by iron columns and rimmed by an iron railing.
    IV. Recently a newspaper editor from the South returned from an eight-week trip through the Caribbean and made a number of recommendations on what we should do to counter the lack of accurate information about the United States.
    V. The need is to be candid about our problems, to be informed on what we are going about them, and to resolve them as expeditiously as possible.
    The CORRECT answer is:
    A. I, II   B. II, III   C. III, IV   D. I, V   E. I, III

7. I. "Man is flying too fast for a world that is round," he said. "Soon he will catch up with himself in a great rear-end collision."
    II. After the raid on the club, each of the men suspected of accepting racetrack bets, along with the owner of the club, were held for questioning at police headquarters.
    III. It seems to me that at the opening performance of the play the audience were of different opinions about its merit and about its chances for a long run.
    IV. Oak from the forests of Vermont and steel from the mills of Pittsburgh are the material of this magnificent modern structure.
    V. The machine is subjected to severe strains which it must withstand and at the same time work easily and rapidly.
    The CORRECT answer is:
    A. I, II   B. II, III   C. IV, V   D. I, V   E. II, V

8. I. We don't have to worry about cutting down on expenses; money is no object in this venture.
    II. And now, my dear, let you and I tell our guests of the plans we have for the future.
    III. For all his errors of the past, no one can or has said that he did not turn out on this occasion a perfectpiece of work.
    IV. Hercule Poirot, when looking for a suspect in the murder case never thought of its being me.
    V. During the interpellation the minister refused to answer any questions concerning his predecessor's conduct of the war.
    The CORRECT answer is:
    A. I, III   B. I, IV, V   C. II, III, IV   D. III, IV   E. II, III

9. I. John Steinbeck received the Nobel Prize only a few years ago for his work of the thirties, work, which now, according to some critics, has lost its timeliness and which never had timelessness.
    II. Respect is shown the flag by no matter when it is displayed, whether it be in the window of a private home or on the pole of a public building.
    III. When dinner was over we strolled through the garden and exclaimed at the beauty of the red gladioluses, the pride of the Jenkinses' gardener.
    IV. Mrs. Cosgrove's gift of $100,000 to the hospitals is only the latest of the many acts of generosity by which she has before now benefited her fellow men.
    V. Am I repeating your question exactly when I say, "How many of you are willing to join me in my attempt to rid America of the traitors who are threatening its freedom"?
    The CORRECT answer is:
    A. I, II, III, IV   B. II, IV   C. II, III, IV
    D. I, IV, V   E. I, II, IV

10. I. Slashing the original 73 projects to 20 with little loss of subject matter in the consolidated schedule, a stalemate was avoided and the work of the Council speeded up.

II. I was particularly struck by the unselfishness of the American school children, many of whom willingly donating their allowances, because they felt that they should help the refugees.
III. As a result of Henry VIII's defiance of the Church of Rome, the ecclesiastical principle of government was substituted by the national.
IV. I wish you had invited me to the concert, for I should have liked particularly to hear Piatigorsky.
V. John will be in the best possible position for getting the most out of his vacation and of making business contacts in new markets.
The CORRECT answer is:
A. I, II, III, IV B. I, II, III, V C. I, II, III
D. III, IV, V E. I, II, III, IV, V

11. I. They took him to be me despite ever so many differences in our appearance and despite his addiction to loquacity.
II. They may have more money, they may have more possessions, but they are not any happier than us, as we and they all know.
III. Either Betty or Bob must have thought the teacher's remarks were addressed to him.
IV. There was present at today's conference—and at next week's conference the same group is expected—representatives of many foreign countries, including Italy, France, England, and Germany.
V. The most important criteria in judging the performance of a pianist is not virtuosity but maturity of interpretation.
The CORRECT answer is:
A. I, IV B. II, III, V C. II, IV, V D. I, III E. I, IV, V

12. I. Thoroughly exhausted after we had swum for six hours, we lay breathless on the sand and oblivious of anything but our utter fatigue.
II. The jury seems in violent disagreement about the culpability of the defendant; such shouting as we hear from the jury room is most unusual among these halls.
III. The difference between the class' average grades for the first week and those for the eighth week, on alternate forms of the same test, were quite insignificant, indicating, we thought, that instruction had been ineffective.
IV. Each tree and each bush give forth a flaming hue such as we have not seen for many seasons in these climes.
V. We met a man whom we thought we had met many years since, when we lived in South Africa.
The CORRECT answer is:
A. III, IV, V B. I, II, V C. III, IV D. I, II E. I, III, IV

13. I. That old friend, whom I met again last night after a lapse of many a year, stands head and shoulders above any person I have ever known.
II. This is one of the finest pictures which have ever been put on canvas, bringing out rare qualities of tone-color, mature interpretation, and virtuosity in execution.
III. Which of them would you prefer to have working for you, considering the inordinate physical and mental demands of the work, him or his brother?

IV. Throughout Saturday and Sunday, the townsfolk took scarcely any notice of the absence of Jed Gorman, believing him to be off on a drunken spree; but on Monday a body was discovered in the river obviously that of the missing handyman.
V. Things being so pleasant as they were, we could not fathom the reason for John leaving so soon after he had started what we considered an excellent job with unlimited opportunities.
The CORRECT answer is:
A. I, V   B. II, III, V   C. II, III   D. II, IV, V   E. I, IV, V

14. I. He is unfailingly polite not only to his superiors and his colleagues but even to those who are in subordinate positions, and, in general, to whoever else he thinks is deserving of kindly consideration.
    II. Without more ado, he took the books off the radiator, where they had lain quite neglected for several days and where their bindings were beginning to grow loose.
    III. We can still include a discussion of the lunchroom situation among the topics, for the agenda have not yet been printed and will not be for another hour or two.
    IV. We knew who would be at the party and who would take us home, but we didn't know who to expect to meet us at the station upon our arrival.
    V. Despite his protestations, we know that the true reason why he was suffering such obvious anguish and failing to do his work was because of marital trouble.
    The CORRECT answer is:
    A. I, III, IV   B. II, III, V   C. I, IV, V   D. I, II   E. IV, V

15. I. A difficult stretch of bad road in addition to a long detour which caused a series of minor motor mishaps, have much delayed our visitor's arrival and have created an awkward situation for us all.
    II. To make the campaign effective, there is posted in every building, in full view of all entrants, one notice of the location of the shelter, and a second notice intended to boost morale and win cooperation.
    III. One day while leading sheep in the desert and musing upon his people's future, the angel of the Lord appeared to Moses.
    IV. Though he plead with the tongue of an angel, he will not ever alter her cold eyes nor trouble her calm fount of speech.
    V. Despite continuous and well-advised and well-directed efforts by each of us, neither he nor I am able to improve the situation.
    The CORRECT answer is:
    A. I, V   B. III, IV, V   C. I, II, III   D. II, III, IV   E. I, III

16. I. Though business has been brisk of late, this kind of appliances have not sold well at all, despite our continuous and concentrated efforts.
    II. The return trip was a desperate one, with time of the essence; and partly blinded by the unexpected snowstorm, the trip was doubly hazardous.
    III. I started on my journey by foot through forest and mountain, after a last warning to be careful about snake bites by my parents—a warning I knew I must heed on that dangerous terrain.

IV. That he was losing to a better man, a man who had worked diligently and a man of impeccable virtue, was a consideration of but small import to him.
V. The precarious state of affairs was aggravated by a new hazard, notwithstanding all our cautions to avoid any change in the situation.

The CORRECT answer is:
   A. I, III, V   B. II, IV   C. IV, V   D. I, II, III   E. II, III

17.
I. Who's responsible for the feeding of his cat and its young, I'd like to know, we or they? If we, let's feed them.
II. The books that had lain on the desk for many weeks were laid in the bookcase, where they lay until picked up by the messenger from the second-handbook shop.
III. You say I merit the award for competence in my duties; but he deserves an award as well as I, for he is as good, without doubt, or even better than I.
IV. The Joneses' car was more luxurious than, but not necessarily as expensive as, the Browns'.
V. Slowly they tiptoed into the living room hoping not to be heard, but we were fully aware of it being they.

The CORRECT answer is:
   A. II, IV   B. I, III, IV   C. I, V   D. I, II, V   E. III, V

18.
I. I shall lay the rug in the sun, where it has laid many times before; and I shall lie in the sun, too, as always I have lain at leisure while the rug has been drying.
II. Though he knew a great deal about printing machinery, he thought, mistakenly, that the new machine could be made to cast type as well as setting it up.
III. Knowledge in several major fields with sympathy for varied points of view make him an excellent choice for student adviser.
IV. You will find the girls' equipment in the teachers' lounge where the boy's father left it at Professor Wills's suggestion.
V. I know that the Burnses have worked for the mill for generations, and that the Smiths have but recently removed from town, but does either of the Norton boys work here?

The CORRECT answer is:
   A. I, II, III   B. II, III, IV   C. I, IV, V   D. III, V   E. I, II, IV

19.
I. I can put two and two together as quick as most mean; but understanding how he, a slow-witted dolt, could achieve so notable a victory over his opponent is one of the things that puzzle and, forevermore, will puzzle me.
II. Besides my two brothers, my sister, and I, there are a cousin and my father's nephew living at home with us.
III. He has lived in the Reno for many years; previously he lived in Chicago for a short space, after he had come from Los Angeles.
IV. Researchers have been baffled for a long time by this statistic, for it contradicts many of their most highly cherished hypotheses.
V. So intense was the heat near the furnace that all the men at work could not carry on; consequently, production came to a halt.

The CORRECT answer is:
A. I, II, IV   B. III, V   C. I, III, IV   D. I, II, V   E. II, V

20. I. If we can escape from our desks for a brief interval, let's you, Henry, and I put in an appearance at the party.
    II. If you persevere in your ambitions, you are likely to achieve at least a modicum of success; if you malinger, you are liable to court failure.
    III. You may find conditions here congenial, but since I neither like he work nor the salary, it is to no avail for you to attempt to persuade me to stay.
    IV. He has never deigned to take a drink with us, his office colleagues, though we know him now for over fifteen years; and he takes an occasional drink, we know, at home and at his golf club,
    V. Though the results of your investigation are at variance with the hypothesis we advanced, I believe you have interpreted these data in the only ways that have scientific validity.
    The CORRECT answer is:
    A. I, II, IV   B. I, II   C. IV, V   D. II, III, V   E. I, III, IV

20.____

21. I. He can't hardly hear anything unless the room is completely quiet.
    II. His attitude seemed perfectly alright to me.
    III. One can't be too careful, can one?
    IV. He is one of those people who believe in the perfectability of man.
    V. His uneasiness is reflected in his unwillingness to compromise on even the smallest point.
    The CORRECT answer is:
    A. II, III, V   B. I, III   C. I, IV, V   D. I, II, IV   E. III, IV

21.____

22. I. "Have you found what you were looking for?" he asked.
    II. "I have never," she insisted, "Seen such careless disregard for the rights of others."
    III. "I found this ticket on the step," he said. "Did you lose it?"
    IV. "In one way I'd like to enter the contest," said Anne; "in another way I'm not too eager."
    V. "Did he say, "I'm coming?"
    The CORRECT answer is:
    A. I, III, IV   B. II, V   C. III, V   D. II, IV   E. I, II, IV

22.____

23. I. Were I the owner of the dog, I'd keep him muzzled.
    II. In the tennis match Don was paired with Bill; Ed, with Al.
    III. He was given an excellent trade-in allowance on his old car.
    IV. Why doesn't this window raise?
    V. The prow of the vessel had almost completely sank by the time the rescuers arrived on the scene.
    The CORRECT answer is:
    A. I, II, V   B. I, IV, V   C. I, II, III   D. II, V   E. IV, V

23.____

24.
   I. Turning the pages rapidly, his glance fell upon a peculiarly worded advertisement.
   II. Turning the pages rapidly, his eyes noticed a peculiarly worded advertisement.
   III. Turning the pages rapidly, he noticed a peculiarly worded advertisement.
   IV. Turning the pages rapidly made him more attentive to the unusual.
   V. Turning the pages rapidly does not guarantee rapid comprehension.
   The CORRECT answer is:
   A. III, IV, V   B. I, II, IV   C. III, V   D. I, II   E. I, II, III

25.
   I. They told us how they had suffered.
   II. It is interesting (a) to the student, (b) to the parent, and (c) to the teacher.
   III. There were blue, green and red banners.
   IV. "Will you help", he asked?
   V. In addition to reproducibility, an attitude scale must meet various other requirements characteristic of scale analysis procedures.
   The CORRECT answer is:
   A. I, II   B. II, III   C. I only   D. IV only   E. IV, V

KEY (CORRECT ANSWERS)

1. C
2. D
3. A
4. E
5. A

6. A
7. E
8. A
9. B
10. B

11. C
12. C
13. D
14. E
15. C

16. D
17. C
18. A
19. E
20. E

21. D
22. B
23. E
24. D
25. D

PREPARING WRITTEN MATERIAL
EXAMINATION SECTION
TEST 1

DIRECTIONS: Each question consists of a sentence which may or may not be an example of good English usage. Examine each sentence, considering grammar, punctuation, spelling, capitalization, and awkwardness. Then choose the correct statement about it from the four choices below it. If the English usage in the sentence given is better than any of the changes suggested in choices B, C, or D, pick choice A. (Do not pick a choice that will change the meaning of the sentence.) *PRINT THE LETTER OF THE CORRECT ANSWER IN THE SPACE AT THE RIGHT.*

1. We attended a staff conference on Wednesday the new safety and fire rules were discussed.   1._____
    A. This is an example of acceptable writing.
    B. The words "safety," "fire," and "rules" should begin with capital letters.
    C. There should be a comma after the word "Wednesday."
    D. There should be a period after the word "Wednesday" and the word "the" should begin with a capital letter.

2. Neither the dictionary or the telephone directory could be found in the office library.   2._____
    A. This is an example of acceptable writing.
    B. The word "or" should be changed to "nor."
    C. The word "library" should be spelled "libery."
    D. The word "neither" should be changed to "either."

3. The report would have been typed correctly if the typist could read the draft.   3._____
    A. This is an example of acceptable writing.
    B. The word "would" should be removed.
    C. The word "have" should be inserted after the word "could."
    D. The word "correctly" should be changed to "correct."

4. The supervisor brought the reports and forms to an employees desk.   4._____
    A. This is an example of acceptable writing.
    B. The word "brought" should be changed to "took."
    C. There should be a comma after the word "reports" and a comma after the word "forms."
    D. The word "employees" should be spelled "employee's."

5. It's important for all the office personnel to submit their vacation schedules on time.   5._____
    A. This is an example of acceptable writing.
    B. The word "It's" should be spelled "Its."
    C. The word "their" should be spelled "they're."
    D. The word "personnel" should be spelled "personal."

109

6. The report, along with the accompanying documents, were submitted for review.
   A. This is an example of acceptable writing.
   B. The words "were submitted" should be changed to "was submitted."
   C. The word "accompanying" should be spelled "accompaning."
   D. The comma after the word "report" should be taken out.

7. If others must use your files, be certain that they understand how the system works, but insist that you do all the filing and refiling.
   A. This is an example of acceptable writing.
   B. There should be a period after the word "works," and the word "but" should start a new sentence.
   C. The words "filing" and "refiling" should be spelled "fileing" and "refileing."
   D. There should be a comma after the word "but."

8. The appeal was not considered because of its late arrival.
   A. This is an example of acceptable writing.
   B. The word "its" should be changed to "it's."
   C. The word "its" should be changed to "the."
   D. The words "late arrival" should be changed to "arrival late."

9. The letter must be read carefully to determine under which subject it should be filed.
   A. This is an example of acceptable writing.
   B. The word "under" should be changed to "at."
   C. The word "determine" should be spelled "determin."
   D. The word "carefuly" should be spelled "carefully."

10. He showed potential as an office manager, but he lacked skill in delegating work.
    A. This is an example of acceptable writing.
    B. The word "delegating" should be spelled "delagating."
    C. The word "potential" should be spelled "potencial."
    D. The words "he lacked" should be changed to "was lacking."

KEY (CORRECT ANSWERS)

1.	D	6.	B
2.	B	7.	A
3.	C	8.	A
4.	D	9.	D
5.	A	10.	A

TEST 2

DIRECTIONS: Each question consists of a sentence which may or may not be an example of good English usage. Examine each sentence, considering grammar, punctuation, spelling, capitalization, and awkwardness. Then choose the correct statement about it from the four choices below it. If the English usage in the sentence given is better than any of the changes suggested in choices B, C, or D, pick choice A. (Do not pick a choice that will change the meaning of the sentence.) *PRINT THE LETTER OF THE CORRECT ANSWER IN THE SPACE AT THE RIGHT.*

1. The supervisor wants that all staff members report to the office at 9:00 A.M.
   A. This is an example of acceptable writing.
   B. The word "that" should be removed and the word "to" should be inserted after the word "members."
   C. There should be a comma after the word "wants" and a comma after the word "office."
   D. The word "wants" should be changed to "want" and the word "shall" should be inserted after the word "members."

2. Every morning the clerk opens the office mail and distributes it.
   A. This is an example of acceptable writing.
   B. The word "opens" should be changed to "open."
   C. The word "mail" should be changed to "letters."
   D. The word "it" should be changed to "them."

3. The secretary typed more fast on a desktop computer than on a laptop computer.
   A. This is an example of acceptable writing.
   B. The words "more fast" should be changed to "faster."
   C. There should be a comma after the words "desktop computer."
   D. The word "than" should be changed to "then."

4. The new stenographer needed a desk a computer, a chair and a blotter.
   A. This is an example of acceptable writing.
   B. The word "blotter" should be spelled "blodder."
   C. The word "stenographer" should begin with a capital letter.
   D. There should be a comma after the word "desk."

5. The recruiting officer said, "There are many different goverment jobs available."
   A. This is an example of acceptable writing.
   B. The word "There" should not be capitalized.
   C. The word "government" should be spelled "government."
   D. The comma after the word "said" should be removed.

6. He can recommend a mechanic whose work is reliable.
   A. This is an example of acceptable writing.
   B. The word "reliable" should be spelled "relyable."
   C. The word "whose" should be spelled "who's."
   D. The word "mechanic should be spelled "mecanic."

111

2 (#2)

7. She typed quickly; like someone who had not a moment to lose. 7.____
   A. This is an example of acceptable writing.
   B. The word "not" should be removed.
   C. The semicolon should be changed to a comma.
   D. The word "quickly" should be placed before instead of after the word "typed."

8. She insisted that she had to much work to do. 8.____
   A. This is an example of acceptable writing.
   B. The word "insisted" should be spelled "incisted."
   C. The word "to" used in front of "much" should be spelled "too."
   D. The word "do" should be changed to "be done."

9. He excepted praise from his supervisor for a job well done. 9.____
   A. This is an example of acceptable writing.
   B. The word "excepted" should be spelled "accepted."
   C. The order of the words "well done" should be changed to "done well."
   D. There should be a comma after the word "supervisor."

10. What appears to be intentional errors in grammar occur several times in the passage. 10.____
    A. This is an example of acceptable writing.
    B. The word "occur" should be spelled "occurr."
    C. The word "appears" should be changed to "appear."
    D. The phrase "several times" should be changed to "from time to time."

KEY (CORRECT ANSWERS)

1.	B	6.	A
2.	A	7.	C
3.	B	8.	C
4.	D	9.	B
5.	C	10.	C

TEST 3

DIRECTIONS: Each question consists of a sentence which may or may not be an example of good English usage. Examine each sentence, considering grammar, punctuation, spelling, capitalization, and awkwardness. Then choose the correct statement about it from the four choices below it. If the English usage in the sentence given is better than any of the changes suggested in choices B, C, or D, pick choice A. (Do not pick a choice that will change the meaning of the sentence.) *PRINT THE LETTER OF THE CORRECT ANSWER IN THE SPACE AT THE RIGHT.*

1. The clerk could have completed the assignment on time if he knows where these materials were located.
   A. This is an example of acceptable writing.
   B. The word "knows" should be replaced by "had known."
   C. The word "were" should be replaced by "had been."
   D. The words "where these materials were located" should be replaced by "the location of these materials."

2. All employees should be given safety training. Not just those who accidents.
   A. This is an example of acceptable writing.
   B. The period after the word "training" should be changed to a colon.
   C. The period after the word "training" should be changed to a semicolon, and the first letter of the word "Not" should be changed to a small "n."
   D. The period after the word "training" should be changed to a comma, and the first letter of the word "Not" should be changed to a small "n."

3. This proposal is designed to promote employee awareness of the suggestion program, to encourage employee participation in the program, and to increase the number of suggestions submitted.
   A. This is an example of acceptable writing.
   B. The word "proposal" should be spelled "proposal."
   C. The words "to increase the number of suggestions submitted" should be changed to "an increase in the number of suggestions is expected."
   D. The word "promote" should be changed to "enhance" and the word "increase" should be changed to "add to."

4. The introduction of inovative managerial techniques should be preceded by careful analysis of the specific circumstances and conditions in each department.
   A. This is an example of acceptable writing.
   B. The word "technique" should be spelled "techneques."
   C. The word "inovative" should be spelled "innovative."
   D. A comma should be placed after the word "circumstances" and after the word "conditions."

5. This occurrence indicates that such criticism embarrasses him. 5._____
    A. This is an example of acceptable writing.
    B. The word "occurrence" should be spelled "occurence."
    C. The word "criticism" should be spelled "critisism."
    D. The word "embarrasses" should be spelled "embarasses."

KEY (CORRECT ANSWERS)

1. B
2. D
3. A
4. C
5. A

BASIC FUNDAMENTALS OF INTERPERSONAL RELATIONSHIPS

TABLE OF CONTENTS

	Page
INSTRUCTIONAL OBJECTIVES	1
CONTENT	1
INTRODUCTION	1
1. Interpersonal Conduct and Behavior on the Job	1
Formal Organization of the Office	2
Office as a Setting for Formal and Informal Relations	2
Office Behavior	2
2. Interpersonal Communication – The Meaning	3
Importance of Face-to-Face Contacts	3
Listening Techniques	3
3. Factors in Interpersonal Communication	3
The Choice of Words of the Conversant	4
How Each Sees Each Other	4
The Right Time and Place	4
The Effect of Past Experience	4
The Effect of Personal Differences	5
4. Defense Mechanisms in Interpersonal Relations	5
Causes for Defense Mechanisms	5
Results of Use of Defense Mechanisms	5
5. Influences of Role Playing in Interpersonal Relations	6
Exploring Superior-Subordinate Relations	6
Interpersonal Relations Achieved Through Simulation	7
6. Measuring Interpersonal Relations	7
Survey of Interpersonal Values	7
Analysis of Interpersonal Behavior	8
STUDENT LEARNING ACTIVITIES	8
TEACHER MANAGEMENT ACTIVITIES	9
EVALUATION QUESTIONS	10

BASIC FUNDAMENTALS OF INTERPERSONAL RELATIONSHIPS

INSTRUCTIONAL OBJECTIVES

1. Ability to distinguish between formal and informal behavior.
2. Ability to identify the important factors in communicating with people.
3. Ability to understand how defense mechanisms affect communication with others.
4. Ability to identify the roles played in effective person-to-person communication.
5. Ability to acquire the human relations skills needed for getting along with others both on and off the job.
6. Ability to establish greater personal effectiveness with others so as to develop better cooperation and superior-subordinate relationships in public-service working situations.
7. Ability to recognize the mutual dependence of individuals on each other.
8. Ability to form positive attitudes toward the worth and dignity of every human being.
9. Ability to become aware of how feelings affect one's own behavior, as well as one's relationships with other people.
10. Ability to use an understanding of human relationships to effectively work with people.
11. Ability to improve communications with others by developing greater effectiveness in dealing with people in the world of public service.

CONTENT

INTRODUCTION

Perhaps the single most important skill that a public-service worker, or anyone for that matter, needs, is the ability to get along with other people. "Person-to-person" relationships are the building blocks of all social interactions between two-individuals. If there is one essential ingredient for success in life, both on and off the job, it is developing greater effectiveness in dealing with people.

The skill of the teacher is critical to the success of this unit. He should establish a permissive and non-threatening group climate in which free communication and behavior can take place. The importance of this unit cannot be over stated. The overall objective is to establish greater personal effectiveness with others and to develop better co-operative and superior-subordinate relationships in the public-service occupations. Obtaining greater "self-awareness" is a large part of this goal. Because interpersonal relations are affected by a variety of factors, some attention should be given initially to basic rules of conduct and behavior on the job.

1. ## INTERPERSONAL CONDUCT AND BEHAVIOR ON THE JOB
   Most public-service agencies have clearly defined rules and regulations. The behavior of the public-service worker is often guided by the established proce-

dures and directives of that individual agency. In many cases, even individual departments or units will have procedures manuals, which regulate conduct and office work.

Formal Organization of the Office

At one point or another, most public-service employees either work directly in an office, or come in frequent contact with other people working in an administrative or staff office. Students should become familiar with the organizational structure of the occupational groups in which they are planning on working. A park worker, for example, must know about the organization of the Parks Department—what kinds of staff or administrative services are provided, what about training, what are the safety rules, what goes into personnel records, etc. Preparing a flow chart of the relationships between different positions in a particular agency is one way of learning about the organization of that office or agency.

Office as a Setting for formal and Informal Relations

It is necessary to become aware of the different kinds of social relations shared with co-workers and the public. Some co-workers, for example, are seen only at work, and others are seen socially after work and/or on weekends. Factors that determine which co-workers become *personal* friends and which are just *work* friends should be considered and discussed.

On the other hand, a public-service worker usually has more formal relationships with the public with whom he comes into contact. Consider the relationships of the preschool teacher's aide and his students, the library helper and his library patrons, the police cadet and the general public, etc. In each of these cases, the public expects the public-service worker to help them with a particular service.

Although the distinction between formal and informal social relationships is not always clear, one should be sensitive to the fact that both kinds of relationships affect the behavior of the public and the public-service employee, Normally, the very organization of the public-service office helps to create a social climate for developing working relationships of a formal nature, and personal relationships with co-workers and the public which are of a more impersonal nature.

Office Behavior

Specific kinds of behavior relate to these formal and informal relationships with other people. Typically, the formal relationship is well prescribed and regulated by procedures or directives. The license interviewer, as an example, has specific questions to ask, and specific information to obtain from the applicant. Their relationship can be described as formal or prescribed by regulation. On the other hand, other office behavior can best be described as informal and non-prescribed (or *free*). Interpersonal relations in this case are often more personal and relaxed by their very nature.

2. INTERPERSONAL COMMUNICATION - THE MEANING

Interpersonal communication can be defined as a two-way flow of information from person-to-person. One cannot Study human relations without examining the constant relationships that man has with other people; the individual does not exist in a vacuum. Most of man's psychological and social needs are met through dealings with other people. In fact, one psychiatrist (Harry Stark Sullivan) has developed a theory of personality based upon interpersonal situations. This viewpoint, known as the *Interpersonal Theory of Psychiatry,* claims that personality is essentially the enduring pattern of continued interpersonal relationships between people. This interpersonal behavior is all that can be observed as personality.

Importance of Face-to-Face Contacts

The very phrase. *Public Service Occupations,* suggests frequent face-to-face contacts with not only the general public, but with co-workers as well. With possibly a few exceptions, practically every public-service employee encounters frequent person-to-person contacts both on and off the job. The ability to get along with people is a very important part of public-service work.

Listening Techniques

Effective listening is a critical part of interpersonal communications. Listening is an active process, requiring not only that one must *pay attention* to what is being said, but that one must also *listen* for the meaning of what is being said. Almost one-half of the total time spent communicating, (reading, writing, speaking, or listening) is spent in listening.

Even though people get considerable practice at listening, they don't do too well at it. Many studies have shown that, on the average, a person retains only about 25 percent of a given speech after only 10 minutes have elapsed. Most people forget three quarters of what they hear in a relatively short period of time. Clearly, people need to improve their listening skills if they are to become more effective in their relations with other people.

3. FACTORS IN INTERPERSONAL COMMUNICATION

There are a number of components that affect the person-to-person relationship. Some of the factors common to both the sender and the receiver in a person-to-person communication are:

The Attitudes and Emotions of the Individuals

For example - two people are shouting and screaming at each other - how effective is their interpersonal communication?

- *The Needs and Wants of the People Communicating*

Both the sender and receiver have unique desires, some open, and some hidden from the other person. These needs can and do strongly influence interpersonal relationships.

- *The Implied Demands of the Sender and Receiver*

  An important factor in interpersonal communications involves requests or demands. How are these demands handled? What are some typical responses to demands? These factors are common to both the sender and the receiver in interpersonal relations and affect the individual behavior of the people communicating.

The Choice of Words of the Conversant

One's choice of words can have a direct bearing on the interpersonal communication. The vocabulary one uses in interpersonal relationships should be appropriate for the occasion. For example, a preschool teacher's aide would not use the same vocabulary in talking to a three-year-old, as she would in talking to the preschool teacher.

How Each Sees the Other

The process of communicating from person-to-person is greatly influenced by the perception that the sender and receiver have of each other. The feelings that a person has toward the other person are reflected in his tone of voice, choice of words, and even in his *body language.* A reference book mentioned in the resource section of this unit, *How to Read a Person Like a Book,* deals with the importance of body language in person-to-person relationships.

The Right Time and Place

Another factor that may be important in interpersonal relationships is the timing of the communication. For example, one of the first things a supervisor should do if he wants to talk over a problem with his subordinate, is ask the question: "Is this the right time and place?" Problems should not generally be discussed in the middle of an office, where other employees, or the public, can hear the discussion. Personal problems should be discussed only in private.

The Effect of Past Experience

In general, the quality of the person-to-person transaction will depend upon the past experience of the individuals. Human beings have acquired most of their opinions, assumptions, and value judgments through their relationships with other people. Past experience not only helps to teach people about effective interpersonal relationships, it is also often responsible for the irrational prejudices that a person displays. A strong bias usually blocks the interpersonal relationship if the subject of the communication concerns that particular bias.

The Effect of Personal Differences

An additional factor in interpersonal communications involves the intelligence and other personal differences of the people communicating. An example of such a personal difference is the *objectivity* of the people involved, as compared with their *subjectivity*. One person may try to be very fair and objective in discussing a point with another person, yet this other person is, at the same time, taking everything personally and being very subjective in his viewpoint. It is almost as if an adult was talking to an angry child.

Such differences can impede the communications flow between two people. In fact, all the factors mentioned in communications should be examined as to whether they block or facilitate interpersonal relationships. *The most effective interpersonal relationships are those that are adult-like in their character.*

4. DEFENSE MECHANISMS IN INTERPERSONAL RELATIONS

Defense mechanisms are attempts to defend the individual from anxiety. They are essentially a reaction to frustration - a self-deception.

Causes for Defense Mechanisms

In order to help understand some of the causes for defense mechanisms, remember the basic human needs:

- *Biological or physiological needs* - hunger, water, rest, etc.
- *Psychological or social needs* - status, security, affection, justice etc.

Fear of failure in any of these basic needs appears to be related to the development of defense mechanisms; attitudes toward failure, in turn, originate out of the fabric of childhood experience. The social and cultural conditions encountered during childhood determine the rewards and controls which fill one's later life. These childhood experiences, and their resultant consequences, affect personality development, the individual's value system, and his definition of acceptable goals.

Individuals who are dominated by the fear of failure may react by using one of these defense mechanisms:

- *Rationalization* - making an impulsive action seem logical.

- *Projection* - assigning one's traits to others.

- *Identification* - assuming someone else's favorite qualities are their own.

Results of Use of Defense Mechanisms

A common factor to all defense mechanisms is their quality of *self-deception*. People cling to their impulses and actions, perhaps disguising them so that they become socially acceptable. Their defense mechanisms can be found in the everyday behavior of most normal people and, of course, have *direct influences* on interpersonal relationships.

A person, for example, who is responsible for a particular job makes a mistake, and the work doesn't get done. When confronted with the problem by his supervisor, the individual puts the blame on someone or something else. This is a very common form of a defense mechanism.

Defense mechanisms can sometimes have *negative influences* on interpersonal communications. They can contribute to the individual forming erroneous opinions about the other person's motives. These mechanisms can alter the perceptions and evaluations made about the individual by other people, Ways to understand these mechanisms must be sought; one solution is to become more aware of the common defense mechanisms, and to become less defensive through greater acceptance of others.

5. THE INFLUENCES OF ROLE-PLAYING IN INTERPERSONAL RELATIONS

Everyone wears a mask and plays a certain role or roles in life. Even if the role one plays is to be himself, that particular form of behavior can still be considered a role. As a public-service employee, one's role is to serve the public. This can be done in a number of ways. Some of the factors involved in public-service roles will be mentioned below:

<u>Exploring Superior-Subordinate Relations</u>

Public-service employees are accountable for their actions. From the entry-level public administrative analysis trainee, to the President of the United States, every public servant must be accountable to either an immediate supervisor, a governing body, or to the public itself. Entry-level public-service employees gain experience and get promoted, but they continue to be subordinates and responsible for their actions, even though they also become supervisors and have people working for them.

Simulation exercises can be developed which will examine the perceptions of the superior by the subordinate. *Authority* and *power* factors may enter in here, as the superior also perceives the subordinate in a particular way. *Dominance* and *need* factors are at work in superior-subordinate relationships, and the style of leadership used *(autocratic, democratic,* or *lassiez-faire,)* is a form of leadership role.

Peer relationships can be explored through simulation exercises. The ways in which co-workers perceive each other and the resultant effect on cooperation is one area to be examined. Ways to establish a climate or environment for effective, cooperative relations should be sought.

It is desirable also to simulate, for better comprehension, interpersonal communications with the general public. Role-playing techniques, which permit the exploration of person-to-person relationships, are highlighted in the following section on simulation exercises.

Interpersonal Relations Achieved Through Simulation

The preparation of students for entry-level public-service occupations must include an opportunity to experience meaningful interpersonal relations. Public-service employees, whether office or field workers, experience personal relationships with other people every day. The initial success of the public-service worker will depend in large measure upon his ability to interact effectively with others in the office or field. Accordingly, a principle objective of simulation exercises for entry-level public-service education is to have the student acquire the necessary interpersonal relations skills that make for success in all public-service occupations.

When developing a model public-service simulation with the principal objective being to improve favorable interpersonal relations, certain criteria must be established. These criteria may be stated as follows:

- *Interpersonal relations must be the principal component of the simulation*. Provision must be made for students to interact with others in an office interpersonal setting so that they may work and communicate effectively with one another.

- *The simulation must be as realistic as possible*. Realism can best be accomplished by simulating an actual public-service operation in as many areas as possible.

- *Originality must play an important part*. Model simulations, currently in use, must not be copied in an effort to maintain simplicity.

- *The simulation must be interesting*. Students must be motivated to participate in the simulation and to be enthusiastic about its operation.

- *The simulation must be unstructured*. Provision must be made to allow for an awareness of events as they take place. Students must learn to cope with a situation without prior knowledge that the situation will occur.

In order for the teacher to determine if the model public-service simulation developed has, in fact, improved interpersonal relations, the simulation must be evaluated in terms of meeting the established objectives.

6. ## MEASURING INTERPERSONAL RELATIONS

   ### Survey of Interpersonal Values

   A valid and reliable instrument for measuring interpersonal relations, such as the *Survey of Interpersonal Values,* may be used for this purpose. This instrument is intended for grades 9-12, and is designed to measure the relative importance of the major factored interpersonal value dimensions. These values include both the subject's relations with others and others with himself. The value dimensions considered are:

   - *Support*--being treated with understanding, encouragement, kindness, and consideration.

   - *Conformity*--doing what is socially correct, accepted, and proper.

- *Recognition*--being admired, looked up to, considered important, and attracting favorable notice.

- *Independence*--being able to do what one wants to do, making one's own decisions, doing things in one's own way.

- *Benevolence*--doing things for other people, sharing, and helping.

- *Leadership*--being in charge of others, having authority or power.

A pretest on interpersonal values is administered before the model public-service simulation actually begins, and the same test is administerd as a post-test after a stipulated period of time. By comparison of results, and through the use of applicable statistics, the gain in behavior modification in interpersonal relations can be determined, as a result of using the model public-service simulation.

Analysis of Interpersonal Behavior

Public-service employees should be aware of their own needs, and of the needs of other people. They should be able to recognize situations or behavior calling for professional help, and be able to refer people to such appropriate help. New employees must be able to use their knowledge of person-to-person relationships to effectively work with people.

In order to become more effective in interpersonal relationships, students must gain an understanding of:

- *Self-evaluation* - to be able to assess their own strengths and weaknesses.

- *Group Evaluation* - as a class to be able to evaluate other individuals' competencies in interpersonal communications.

- *Correction of own self-perception* - to be able to do something about the knowledge and attitudes formed by adjusting their individual behavior.

STUDENT LEARNING ACTIVITIES

- Define formal and informal social behavior.

- List the important factors in interpersonal communication.

- View and discuss the film strip, *Your Educational Goals, No. 2: Human Relationships.*

- Role play in alternate supervisor-subordinate relationships practicing effective interpersonal communication.

- Write an essay on "Defense mechanisms affect interpersonal relationships."

- View the film, *The Unanswered Question,* and discuss human relationships afterwards.

- Listen to a discussion of structured interpersonal communications and evaluate the effectiveness of the person-to-person relationship.

- In small groups, discuss the ways in which people are mutually dependent on each other,
- Use simulation exercises to practice interpersonal relations.
- List the different kinds of roles and games played in interpersonal communications.
- Debate the statement: *Understanding person-to-person relations is one of the most important skills a person can acquire for success in life.*
- Discuss how understanding interpersonal relationships can help a person to effectively work with people.
- Define the role of recognizing one's own feelings in relation to others.

TEACHER MANAGEMENT ACTIVITIES

- Have the students define formal and informal social behavior.
- Show transparencies on interpersonal relations, *(Social Sensitivity Iour Relationship with Others)* and discuss concepts afterwards.
- Assign written exercises on the important factors in interpersonal communication.
- Set up role-playing exercises on subordinate-supervisor roles in effective interpersonal communication.
- Encourage small-group discussions of the ways people are mutually dependent on each other.
- Show a movie on human relationships *(The Unanswered Question)* and discuss key points afterwards.
- Separate the class into teams to debate such statements as: Understanding interpersonal relations is one of the most important skills a person can acquire for success in life.
- Encourage individual study and reading in interpersonal relationships.
- Assign an essay on the worth and dignity of man in interpersonal relations.
- Bring in public-service workers who deal with others to talk to the class about the value of effective interpersonal communications.

Evaluation Questions

Fill in the crossword puzzle below.

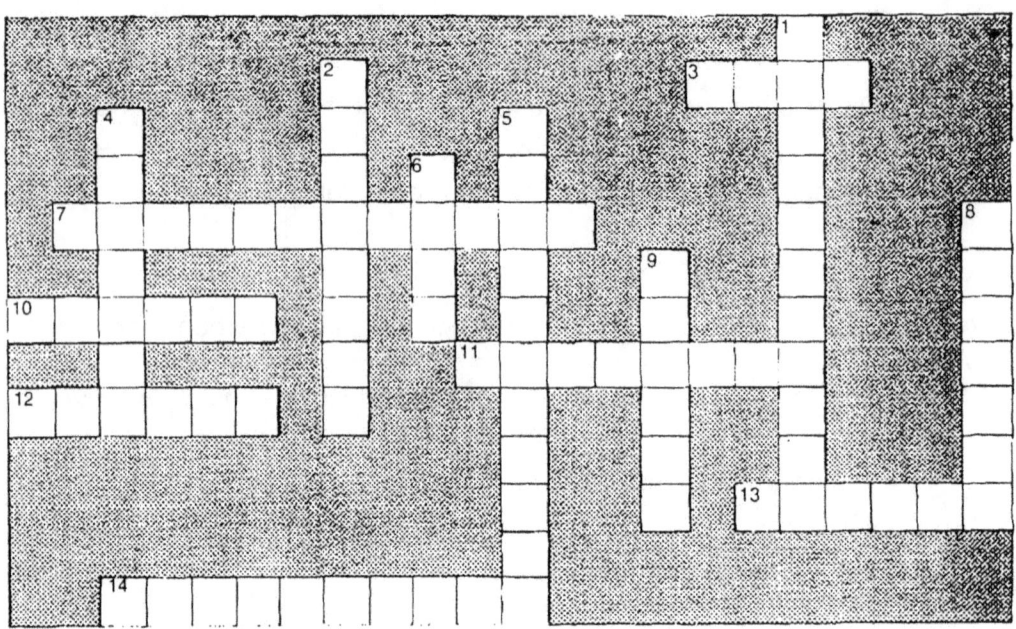

ACROSS:
3. A strong prejudice or _____ can block good relationships.
7. Being able to do what one wants to do satisfies the need for _____.
10. One's _____ of words should be correct for the occasion.
11. Friends usually have an _____ relationship.
12. In talking over problems with others, _____ is important.
13. Everyone needs to feel _____.
14. _____ is assigning one's traits to others.

DOWN:
1. We _____ when we try to make our actions seem logical.
2. When we assume someone's qualities as our own we _____ with that person.
4. Individuals _____ when they do what is socially proper.
5. When we attract favorable attention, we gain _____.
6. Some people have a strong _____ of failure.
8. _____ mechanics help to protect a person from anxiety.
9. A public service worker usually has a _____ relationship with the public.

Answer Key

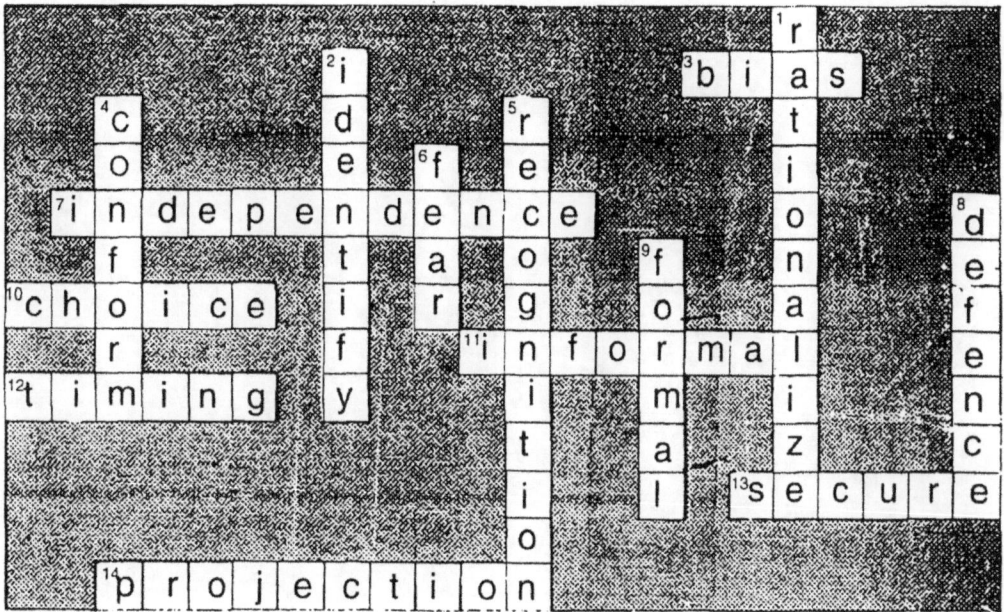